ENCLOSURE AND POPULATION

PIONEERS OF DEMOGRAPHY

A series of collective reprints of the more important milestones in the development of historical demography.

THIS SERIES INCLUDES:

The earliest classics: John Graunt and Gregory King
Mortality in pre-industrial times: the contemporary verdict
Enclosure and population
The population of Ireland before the 19th century
Population and disease in early industrial England
Comparative statistics in the 19th century
Slum conditions in London and Dublin
Mortality in mid 19th century Britain
Rates of mortality
J.-B. Bertrand: *A historical relation of the plague at Marseilles in the year 1720*
T. Short: *Comparative history of the increase and decrease of mankind*
T. Short: *New observations on city, town and country bills of mortality*
W. Black: *An arithmetical and medical analysis of the diseases and mortality of the human species*
E. H. Greenhow: *Papers relating to the sanitary state of the people of England* (General Board of Health Papers)

Each volume contains a new introduction.

ENCLOSURE AND POPULATION

J. Howlett

AN ENQUIRY INTO THE INFLUENCE

WHICH ENCLOSURES HAVE HAD

UPON THE POPULATION OF ENGLAND

1786

*

ENCLOSURES, A CAUSE OF IMPROVED AGRICULTURE,

OF PLENTY AND CHEAPNESS OF PROVISIONS

1787

With an introduction

by

A. H. JOHN

1973

GREGG INTERNATIONAL PUBLISHERS LIMITED

ISBN 0 576 53285 1

Printed in Germany

INTRODUCTION

Not much is known about John Howlett's origins or, indeed, about his early career. Born in 1731, the son of another John Howlett of Bedworth, Warwickshire, he matriculated at St. Edmund Hall, Oxford in November 1749, but graduated in 1755 as a student of St. John's College.[1] The next twenty-five years of his life remain something of a mystery. He seems to have played little further part in university life, taking his master's degree only in 1795, towards the end of his life, and his B.D. degree in 1796. He was evidently living in Maidstone in 1781, the place of publication of his first works and the address given in a letter to Arthur Young in that year. He was not, however, a beneficed clergyman in the town but may have had either independent means, or employment as a schoolmaster or private tutor. What is certain is that he seems to have established a circle of influential friends by this date, including Arthur Young, the Bishop of Chester, and Lord Loughborough who contributed the appendix to his first book. In 1782, possibly helped by his newly acquired reputation as a political arithmetician, Howlett was appointed to the parish of Great Dunmow, Essex, by the Bishop of London. This was a valuable and conveniently situated living, whose stipend Howlett was able to augment by a further appointment as vicar of Badow in 1786. For the rest of his life, he combined parish duties with a good deal of writing and travelling. He toured France in the summer of 1787 with 'very agreeable companions,'[2] for example, and was constantly about the southern parts of England. It was on one such visit that he died at Bath in February, 1804, in his 73rd year.

An Examination of Dr. Price's Essay on the Population of England and Wales appeared in 1781 when Howlett was fifty years of age, the first of a spate of further publications which reveal him as a man of ready pen, of an independent and analytical frame of mind, and a tenacious controversialist. His views reflected much of what Hazlitt has called 'the Spirit of the Age'. As a man of the Enlightenment, Howlett had a typically cool, rational approach to religion; and held to the *tabula rasa* theory of the mind whereby all men are thought to be born intrinsically equal. Like others of his generation he shared in the changed attitudes to the poor, believing in the need to educate them and in the incentive effect of high wages. More generally, he was greatly influenced by the work of Adam Smith and Arthur Young, although without totally accepting their ideas. In his use of statistical material and deduction from observed fact, Howlett mirrored two important features of contemporary thought which, in political arithmetic as in technology and science, had their origins in the preceding century. He drew his evidence from a wide knowledge of the published works in both English and French, supplemented by that obtained through travel and correspondence. As a political arithmetician, he worked in the related fields of demography, poor law and agriculture, the focus of his interests moving, after the middle of the 1780s, from population problems to those of poverty and farming, although rarely overlooking their demographic implications. Here, he shared most of the views of the agricultural reformers of the day—the necessity for enclosure and a general enclosure bill, the greater efficiency of large farms and the need for long leases. He differed from them in opposing the commutation of tithes and, following Adam Smith, was sceptical of some aspects of the Corn Laws. He became a frequent contributor to Young's *Annals of Agriculture* and by 1790 was among its regular county correspondents. At the time of his death, Howlett was engaged on a report on Essex farming for the Board of Agriculture, subsequently completed by Young and published in 1808.

What first stimulated Howlett's intervention in the demographic controversy of the second half of the eighteenth century is not known; but it could well have been the earlier works of Arthur Young. The appearance of his *Examination of Dr. Price's Essay* in 1781 brought him into immediate prominence as a critic of this established figure for whom wars, the growth of towns and developments in agriculture spelt a declining population. By contrast, Howlett held that the population of England and Wales had virtually doubled since 1688 and, further, that the rate of increase was accelerating. Two estimates of the population of England and Wales were calculated for the year 1780: that based on the Window Tax reaching 8.69m and the other, on different evidence, 7.9m. The first of these was subsequently retracted, 'it being founded on an entire misconception of the manner in which the district and county surveyors make their collective returns of cottages.' The second was also revised many years later and reduced to 7.5m.[3] His views, however, were critically received, and the two essays reprinted here were, in effect, attempts to reinforce his arguments. But he lived just long enough for the census of 1801 to confirm his major contention, and his revised estimate of numbers in 1780 has not been improved upon.

It might have been expected that this statistical work would have been followed by an extended investigation into the reasons for population growth, but this was never attempted. Instead, Howlett's views on this crucial question have to be pieced together from his various writings. These indicate that he believed both a fall in mortality and a rise in fertility were important and that their significance varied from region to region. In this he was less dogmatic than most of his contemporaries for whom the rise in fertility was the major reason for the increase in numbers.

Judging by his sombre account of the conditions of rural labour in Essex—a county virtually unaffected by eighteenth-century enclosure and with a declining woollen industry–this lack of dogmatism may have arisen from his inability to fit the local situation into a simple framework of explanation. There appeared to be no obvious reasons for either a fall in mortality or a rise in fertility. Yet, because of rising numbers, an inadequate demand for labour and higher food prices 'our poor', he wrote in 1788, 'are certainly poorer, and have been so for the past twenty years, than they have been in any former time.'[4] Under-employment was widespread, about a third of the rural workers needing occasional support from the poor law. It was in Howlett's view, a 'popular error that the proportion of poor in large cities and populous manufacturing towns, is higher than in mere agricultural country parishes; where the fact is just the contrary.'[5] In particular, the wages paid to labourers in and about Manchester were double those current in his part of Essex. Rising food prices made matters worse; and potatoes were increasingly supplementing bread in the diet of the poor. He might well have reflected that the widening range of food could have been a factor in the fall of mortality. Even the poor had potatoes where earlier they had depended on vetches and similar greenstuffs plucked from the fields and hedgerows. Unlike Malthus, he supported a generous poor relief policy; he opposed the Speenhamland System and favoured the establishment of a legal minimum wage.

His belief in the fall in mortality largely rested on the effects of inoculation. Writing to Arthur Young in 1781, soon after the publication of *An Examination of Dr. Price's Essay*, Howlett reported

> I am collecting fresh material and am already furnished with no inconsiderable Variety, not only more fully and amply to establish the Idea of an increased and increasing population among us but of diminished mortality, a Consideration of great and pleasing Importance, and in which I think I have your entire Concurrence. I shall chiefly confine myself to the difference in this respect that has been occasioned by the Practice of Innoculation; which is mostly to be sought for in large provincial Towns and considerable populous Villages, tho' sometimes likewise to be found even in scattered Country parishes.[6]

Part of this evidence appeared in his *Observations on the Increased Population, Healthiness etc. of the Town of Maidstone* (1782), where attention was drawn to the remarkable decline in the number of deaths from smallpox with the widening use of inoculation after 1760.[7] The significance of contagious and infectious diseases in areas of high population density, implied in the letter to Young, was later used as an argument against Gilbert's Act of 1782, allowing parishes to combine for the purpose of building houses of industry. Mortality generally, according to Howlett, was higher in these institutions during outbreaks of measles, smallpox and putrid fever than among the poor relieved at home. Nothing was written about the state of medicine and medical care in this country; though he was less than complimentary about the *Hotel Dieu* in Paris, dubbing it as 'that celebrated slaughter house.'[8] He thus anticipated many of the modern ideas on the subject.

To deal with the fall in mortality in this way was unusual for the time; but, apart from the remarks on Maidstone, Howlett does not seem to have developed the theme. He was much more in accord with contemporary thinking in treating the factors underlying an increase in fertility. 'Most writers from Adam Smith to Malthus believed that population growth was determined by the demand for labour; an increase in the demand for labour raised wages or made it easier to find employment, and in either case it enabled the labourer to marry earlier'[9] and possibly influenced the number ultimately marrying. Both meant more children; and, as far as earlier marriages are concerned, the shorter interval between generations also meant a greater 'number born in a given period of time.'[10] Consequent changes in the age-structure of the population would further tend towards a larger population. The demand for labour, in turn, was determined by the volume of investment in industry and agriculture, so linking the growing economy with a bigger population. 'The demand for men like that for any other commodity', in Adam Smith's words, 'necessarily regulates the production of men.'

Enclosure, to the minds of most agricultural reformers, was an inclusive term for this investment in the farming sector, involving both re-organisation of land and its subsequent more intensive cultivation. They were aware too of its indirect effects upon employment in the processing and distribution of a larger farm output and, because of a rising demand for implements and other items, in industry also. Howlett accepted these hypotheses in an interestingly guarded way; enclosures had 'not only augmented our numbers, but even more augmented them than any other cause in similar situations.'[11] They explain his belief that the proportion of the poor was lower in the 'cities and populous manufacturing towns' than in the countryside, as well as the arguments which underlie the pamphlets reprinted in this volume. Of the other possible, but more subtle, effects of enclosure upon the rise in fertility—the shift from owner-occupancy to tenancy, the decline in the practice of boarding farm workers and the more complete proletarianisation of agricultural labours—Howlett had nothing to say.

Proof that enclosures 'augmented our numbers' was attempted in two essentially complementary ways in these essays. *An Enquiry into the Influence which Enclosures have had upon the Population of this Kingdom* is demographic in its approach, using material drawn from the Anglican parish registers and the return of men for militia duty in the county of Rutland. To the modern reader, the result is not particularly convincing, partly because of the intrinsic deficiencies of the evidence used, partly because—as Howlett later admitted—his sample of newly enclosed parishes was hardly big enough.[12] *Enclosures, a cause of Improved Agriculture, of Plenty and Cheapness of Provisions*, which is something of a *tour de force*, sets out to demonstrate the greater productivity of enclosed areas, especially the wastes, and from that argues to a greater demand for labour. Intellectually, it is the more forceful of the two essays, shewing great skill in economic argument.

More recent work would agree with Howlett that enclosure increased the demand for labour and, over-all, did not cause depopulation. The immediate business of re-dividing the land, often involving ditching, and road-building, obviously increased work in the short-run; while in the long-run the extent to which this occurred depended upon the kind of land enclosed and the type of farming subsequently pursued. On the first of these, historians are handicapped by a lack of adequate enclosure statistics. But, it seems probable that at least as great an area of wastes was enclosed as of openfield between 1740 and 1815. If so, then clearly there was much building in addition to the other ways in which employment was increased. The more intensive cultivation of the wastes thus almost certainly increased the demand for labour irrespective of the kind of farming pursued after enclosure. Even where enclosure led to the conversion of arable to pasture—the basic theme of contemporary complaint—it is by no means certain that depopulation followed. Chambers has argued that here too there was more work because the system used was not that of permanent pasture but an arable form of grass farming and also because output increased faster than labour saving innovations.[13]

The weakness of Howlett's position, however, is that the local coincidence of enclosure and increased numbers does not necessarily imply a causal relationship as he, and others of the time, assumed it did. No evidence is produced to substantiate increased fertility or to prove that this was the most important factor underlying the growing population of newly enclosed parishes. And this remains a weakness with regard to the role of fertility in eighteenth-century population growth. It is still true that 'with the exception of some indications of moderately rising fertility in a single Devon village and within the peerage,'[14] little is known with any degree of certainty. Hence the relationship between increased demand for labour and the age of marriage, though plausible, remains strictly unproven, as also do the other suggested effects of enclosure upon the birthrate. Further, Colyton, the Devon village for which there is reasonably good evidence of rising fertility after 1750, was a parish of small farms enclosed during medieval times. Other factors than enclosure must evidently have affected rural fertility, including possibly non-economic factors.

Howlett thus remains an interesting writer on the demographic history of the eighteenth century in the sense that many of his ideas are still relevant to present day discussions. Time has eroded much of the reputation which he achieved in his lifetime: 'the nation at large are much indebted to this writer,' wrote a reviewer in *The Gentleman's Magazine*, 'for his attention to agriculture and population, and the effects of enclosures, poor rates and tithes on both.'[15] But he retains much merit as an acute commentator on many of the pressing problems of his day.

A. H. John
September 1972

A List of Publications by John Howlett

An Examination of Dr. Price's Essay on the Population of England and Wales; (Maidstone, 1781)

Observations on the increased population, healthiness etc. of the Town of Maidstone; (Maidstone, 1782)

Reply to letter on Howlett's 'Examination of Dr. Price's Essay'; *Gentleman's Magazine*, vol. 52 (1782), p. 473

An Enquiry into the Influence which Enclosures have had upon the Population of England; (London, 1786)

An Essay on the Population of Ireland; (London, 1786)

Confirmation: A Sermon preached at the visitation of the Right Reverend the Bishop of London, in the Church of Thaxted, in Essex, on Friday, May 26, 1786

Enclosures a cause of Improved Agriculture [by a Country Farmer]; (London, 1787)

The Insufficiency of the causes to which the Increase of our Poor and the Poor's Rates have been generally ascribed; (London, 1788)

'On the Population of Cavenham', *Annals of Agriculture*, IX (1788), p. 113

'On the Provision for the Poor', *Annals of Agriculture*, IX (1789), p. 1

'Reply to a letter from Mr. Erskine on the Poor', *Annals of Agriculture*, XIV (1790), p. 174

'Reply to circular on agricultural prices', *Annals of Agriculture*, XV (1791), p. 260

'On the Population of France', *Annals of Agriculture*, XV (1791), p. 537

'The different Quantity and Expence of Agricultural Labour in different Years', *Annals of Agriculture*, XVIII (1792), p. 566

'On the Population and Situation of the Poor in England', *Annals of Agriculture*, XVIII (1792), p. 573

Great Welnetham; *Annals of Agriculture*, XXI (1793), p. 108

Parish of Welnetham; *Annals of Agriculture*, XXI (1793), p. 377

Reply to circular on the state of the crops and condition of the poor; *Annals of Agriculture*, XXIV (1795), p. 154

Reply to circular on the state of the crops; *Annals of Agriculture*, XXV (1796), p. 599

An Examination of Mr. Pitt's Speech in the House of Commons on 12th February 1796, relative to the condition of the Poor, (London, 1796)

Dispersion of the present gloomy apprehensions of late repeatedly suggested by the Decline of our Corn Trade, (London, 1797)

Reply to circular on the number and use of horses; *Annals of Agriculture*, XXVIII (1797), p. 410

An Enquiry concerning the Influence of Tithes upon Agriculture; *with remarks on Arthur Young*, (London, 1797)

The Monthly Reviewers reviewed in a letter to those Gentlemen, pointing out their Misrepresentations and fallacious Reasonings in the Account of the Pamphlet 'Dispersion of the . . . apprehensions . . .', (London, 1798)
The Sword of the Lord and of Gideon, a sermon preached in his parish church before the Volunteer Corps of Yoeman Cavalry, September 11th, 1798
Reply to circular respecting the commutation of tithes etc.; *Annals of Agriculture*, XXXII (1799), p. 414
'Influence of Tithes on Agriculture', *Annals of Agriculture*, XXXVIII (1802), p. 131

Other Works Containing Writings by John Howlett

Isaac Wood, *Some Account of Shrewsbury House of Industry* (1792) [Appendix —a correspondence with Howlett]
J. Middleton, *A view of the Agriculture of Middlesex*, (London, 1798) [A letter from Howlett]
Arthur Young, *A General View of the Agriculture of the County of Essex* (London, 1807) [Quotes extensively from an unpublished report by Howlett]

1 *The Gentleman's Magazine* LXXIV (1804) Pt. I, p. 282.

2 B.M. Add. MSS 35126, f.409 Letter dated 15.XI.1787.

3 John Middleton, *View of The Agriculture of Middlesex* (London, 1798), p. 563. Republished in *The Population Controversy* by Gregg International Publishers Limited, Farnborough, England, 1973.

4 John Howlett, *The Insufficiency of the Causes to which the Increase of our Poor and of the Poor Rates have been commonly ascribed* (London, 1788), p. 28.

5 John Howlett, *Annals of Agriculture*, XX (1789), p. 6

6 B.M. Add. MSS 35126, f.195. Letter dated 4.VII.1781.

7 *Observations on the Increased Population, Healthiness etc. of the Town of Maidstone* (Maidstone, 1782), pp. 7–8. Republished in *Development of Population Statistics* by Gregg International Publishers Limited, Farnborough England, 1973.

8 *Annals of Agriculture* XV (1791), p. 540.

9 H. J. Habakkuk, *Population Growth and Economic Development since 1750* (Leicester, 1971), p. 39.

10 H. J Habakkuk, *Population Growth and Economic Development since 1750* (Leicester, 1971), pp. 37–8.

11 John Howlett, *Enclosures, a cause of Improved Agriculture of Plenty and Cheapness of Provisions* (London, 1787), p. 1.

12 *Enclosures a cause of Improved Agriculture* (London, 1787), p. 1.

13 J. D. Chambers, 'Enclosure and the Labour Supply in the Industrial Revolution', *Economic History Review*, 2nd Series V, (1953).

14 M. L. Flinn, *British Population Growth 1700–1850* (London, 1970), p. 36.

15 *Gentleman's Magazine* LXXII (1802), p. 435.

ENQUIRY
INTO THE
INFLUENCE
WHICH
ENCLOSURES
HAVE HAD UPON THE
POPULATION
OF THIS
KINGDOM.

By the Reverend J. HOWLETT,
Vicar of GREAT DUNMOW, ESSEX.

SECOND EDITION.

To which is added an

APPENDIX,

CONTAINING

A LETTER from the Rev. J. CHAPPEL WOODHOUSE, Rector of DONINGTON, in SHROPSHIRE; which ſtrongly illuſtrates the neceſſary Increaſe of People from an improved Agriculture in general, and from Encloſures in particular.

LONDON:
Printed for W. RICHARDSON, Royal Exchange.
M DCC LXXXVI.

Republished in 1973 by Gregg International Publishers Limited
Westmead, Farnborough, Hants, England

A N

E N Q U I R Y, &c.

SCARCELY any thing at all connected with the improvements of modern agriculture, has been more eagerly contested, or more amply discussed, than the advantages or disadvantages of Enclosures with respect to their influence on Population. Dr. Price has uniformly maintained their immediate and powerful tendency to depopulate, and has printed and reprinted accounts to confirm and eſtabliſh this idea, without ſeeming to have at all attended to the accounts, of equal authenticity, repeatedly given on the other ſide of the queſtion. Such partial repreſentations are only calculated to miſlead. In his late edition of Reverſionary Payments, after a diſmal detail of the pernicious conſequences of Encloſures, (Vol. II. p. 269.) he obſerves, that he can ſcarcely think of any thing that ſhould be more alarming, and exclaims, "How aſto-"niſhing is it, that our Parliament, "inſtead of applying any remedy to "theſe evils, ſhould chuſe to promote "them, by paſſing, every year, bills al-"moſt without number for new Enclo-"ſures!"

" ſures!" If the accounts he had given were not only true, but ſtated in all their attendant circumſtances and effects, and the ſame were ſtrictly applicable to all, or only the greater part of, the Encloſures which have taken place during the laſt thirty years, there would, indeed, be ſome foundation for ſuch complaints and exclamations; and we could not form any very favourable conception of the judgment or patriotiſm of our ſucceſſive repreſentatives. But before we admit concluſions ſo very diſhonourable to any part of our legiſlature, let us fairly examine the ſeveral articles of the Doctor's information, as well as that given by others of a different and oppoſite tenour.

And firſt, as to the Doctor's communications; he tells us, Vol. II. p. 267. that "he had lately received "an account of a large common-field "in Leiceſterſhire, which uſed to produce 800 quarters of corn, beſides "maintaining 200 cattle, which now, "in conſequence of being incloſed, and "getting into fewer hands, produces "little or no corn, and maintains no "more cattle than before, though the "rents are conſiderably advanced." This account ſeems to carry its own refutation along with it. It had alſo been printed before, and, in my apprehenſion,

prehension, satisfactorily answered by Mr. Arthur Young, in his Political Arithmetick, p. 146. "If the Doc-"tor," says he, "had formed his "tables on no better authority than "this, they would not have been "very famous. *Rents raised,——corn "disappeared,——cattle not increased!* "What are we to think of such *facts?* "I travelled through Leicestershire "and Northamptonshire, and not, I "think, without attention. I saw "great tracts of country enclosed and "laid from arable to grass; but I saw "in the graziers fields such herds of "fat sheep and oxen, as delighted "the eye.—The generality of these

"lands

"lands are ſtocked at the rate of a "large ox, and 2½ ſheep to every two "acres; and the ſoil does ſo well in "graſs, that they fat large ſheep the "winter through. Before the Enclo- "ſure, thoſe lands were managed in "the courſe of fallow, wheat, and "ſpring-corn. How, in the name of "wonder, were fat ſheep and oxen "then kept?—Upon the fallows?— "or upon ſtraw? That corn diſap- "pears is moſt certain, but that it "is amply made up by beef and "mutton is equally certain." This is ſurely, to ſay the leaſt of it, as good and ſatisfactory information as the Doctor's.

But the Doctor further informs us, *from the Reverend Mr. Addington's Enquiry into the Reasons for and against enclosing open Fields, published in* 1772, *for Mr. Buckland, Pater-noster Row,* "that the new inclosed lordships are "turned into pasturage; in conse-"quence of which many lordships "have now not 50 acres ploughed "yearly, in which 1500, or at least "1000 were ploughed formerly; and "scarce an ear of corn is now to be "seen in some that bore hundreds of "quarters." Granting all this to be true, it naturally occurs, how many more sheep and oxen were now fed and fattened than before? How much more beef and mutton produced?

What greater quantities of wool, hides, tallow, &c. how many hands employed in manufacturing these? How many persons, in different places, clothed, fed, and supported? This we are not informed, and yet without this, all the rest, as far as population is concerned, and indeed even tillage, in other quarters, conveys very little instruction. "But," continues Mr. Addington, "the effects of these En-"closures are so severely felt, that "worse wheat has lately been sold "in these counties of Leicester and "Northampton, on an average at 7s. "or 7s. 6d. the Winchester bushel, "for many months together, than "used to be sold for 3s. 6d. or 4s."

How

How extremely little is all this to the purpoſe! Who does not know that in the beſt corn counties in the kingdom, where there has been neither recent incloſures, nor converſion of tillage into paſture, wheat has been ſold, for months together, not only at 7s. a buſhel, but even 8 or 9s. of an inferior quality likewiſe to what was purchaſed the year *before*, or perhaps the year *after*, not merely for 3 or 4s. but half a crown? But ſuppoſing the above extravagant price of grain to be the *permanent* effect of the Encloſures, and of the conſequent exchange of tillage for paſture, the evil would very ſoon cure itſelf. The farmer, confident of the vaſt advantage of growing corn, would ſell off his ſheep and oxen, break up his meadows, ſow them with wheat, and in *the room of* 50 *acres, you would ſoon again have* 1500 *and* 1000 *buſhels of corn for a ſingle ear.*

But what immediately follows in the ſame writer is more directly to the preſent purpoſe. " The decreaſe " of *inhabitants,* in almoſt all the en- " cloſed villages," ſays he, " in which " they have no conſiderable manufac- " ture, is obvious to be remarked by " every one who knew their ſtate " 20 or 30 years ago, and ſees them " now. The ruin of former dwelling- " houſes, barns, ſtables, &c. ſhews

" every

" every one who paſſes through them " that they were once better inhabited. " A hundred houſes and families " have dwindled into eight or ten. " The land-holders are very few in " moſt pariſhes that have been encloſed " only 15 or 20 years, in compariſon " of the numbers, which occupied " them in their open field ſtate. It " is no uncommon thing to ſee four " or five wealthy graziers engroſſing a " large encloſed lordſhip, which was " before in the hands of 20 or 30 " farmers, and as many ſmaller tenants " and proprietors; all theſe are hereby " thrown out of their livings, with " their families, that were employed or " ſupported by them." All this may be very true; and the following account, which I myſelf received from a correſpondent in Leiceſterſhire, of ſimilar purport, is ſtill more pointed and determinate. "As to Encloſures," ſays he, "I can mention two "villages in this county within two "miles of each other, *Wiſtow* and "*Foſton*, which formerly contained 34 "or 35 dwellings; but by Encloſure, "*Foſton* is reduced to three habita-"tions; the parſonage-houſe accom-"modates one family, and the two "other buildings are occupied by "ſhepherds, who manage the ſtock "for their diſtant renters, as the whole "lordſhip belongs to one perſon. "And as to *Wiſtow*, the 34 manſions

" have vanifhed in a very few years, " and no dwelling remains but the " late Sir Charles Halford's hall-houfe, " who owned the lordfhip; and thefe " are called improvements; for double " and treble rents enfue, and double " or treble the old value of land and " houfe rents, and fo of *provifions*." What became, it is natural to afk, of thefe *vanifhed inhabitants*, and who took off thefe *increafed provifions?* My correfpondent has clearly fuggefted the anfwer in another part of his letter, and which is, indeed, equally applicable to the preceding account, given by Dr. Price from Mr. Addington. " Manufacture," fays he, " has " *overpeopled* Leicefterfhire. Almoft

" every

"every village uninclosed is chiefly "inhabited by Woolcombers, and "Frame-work Knitters; and though "we possess a rich soil, Rutland and "Northamptonshire corn arrives in vast "quantities; and is usually very reason-"able, as well as butter. But cheese, "notwithstanding a vast produce of "our own, is swept away at our "fairs by factors, and is rather dear." This needs no comment; the conclusions are obvious; diminution of tillage and inhabitants in one place; the consequent increase of them in another; the multiplication of sheep and oxen in the County of Leicester, brings corn in abundance from those of Northampton and Rutland, and no article remains

dear,

dear, but that produced on the ſpot, which is ſent off to fill the multiplied mouths in other quarters.

Similar intelligence to the above I could produce from letters now lying before me with regard to incloſures in the Counties of *Bucks*, *Bedford*, *Derby*, *Wilts*, *Hants*, *&c.* but the detail would be tedious, and I muſt beg leave to obſerve, that for one account of this diſadvantageous kind, I have, I believe, two or three of a directly oppoſite tenour, in which the increaſe of inhabitants from incloſures is aſſerted and proved. Inſtead, however, of both the one and the other, I ſhall only give a few Paſſages from Mr. Arthur

Young,

Young, which may ſerve as a contraſt to all the above unfavourable ſtatements, and which may juſtly lay claim to particular credit and attention, as coming from a perſon of more extenſive obſervation in theſe matters than, perhaps, any other man in England, and to whoſe many valuable publications, reſpecting agricultural improvements, this kingdom is under the higheſt obligation.

" It may be laid down as a maxim," ſays he, " Pol. Arith. P. 198, that " without Incloſures there can be no " good huſbandry : while a country is " laid out in open fields, every farmer " tied down to the huſbandry of his

" ſlovenly

" flovenly neighbour, it is fimply im-
" poffible that agriculture fhould flou-
" rifh." And in p. 149, he obferves,
" Dr. Price and the other Writers who
" affure us we fhould throw down our
" hedges, and wafte one third of our
" farms in a barren fallow, by way
" of making beef and mutton cheap,
" will confine themfelves to the In-
" clofures that have converted arable
" to grafs: What fay they to thofe
" which have changed grafs to ara-
" ble? They choofe to be filent. I
" do not comprehend the amufement
" that is found in conftantly looking
" at thofe objects which are fuppofed
" to be gloomy, and in regularly la-
" menting the evils that furround us,

" though they flow from cauſes which " ſhower down much ſuperior bleſ- " ſings. When I look around me in " this country, I think I every where " ſee ſo great and animating a pro- " ſpect, that the ſmall ſpecks which " may be diſcerned in the hemiſphere " are loſt in the brilliancy that ſur- " rounds them. I cannot ſpread a cur- " tain over the illumined ſcene, and " leave nothing to view but the mere " ſhades of ſo ſplendid a ſcene.

" What will theſe Gentlemen ſay " to the Encloſures in Norfolk, Suf- " folk, Nottinghamſhire, Derbyſhire, " Lincolnſhire, Yorkſhire, and all the " Northern Counties? What ſay they

" to

" to the Sands of Norfolk, Suffolk, " Nottinghamſhire, which yield corn, " and mutton, and beef, by the force " of *Encloſure* alone? What ſay they " to the wolds of York and Lincoln, " which from barren heaths at 1s. an " acre, are, by Encloſure alone, render- " ed profitable farms? Aſk Sir Cecil " Wray, if, without Encloſure, he " could advance his heaths by ſan- " foine from 1s. to 20s. an acre? " What ſay they to the vaſt tracts in " the Peak of Derby, which by *En- " cloſure alone*, are changed from black " regions of Ling, to fertile fields " covered with cattle? What ſay they " to the improvement of moors in the

" northern counties, where Enclosures " alone have made those counties smile " with culture, which before were " dreary as night? What have these " gentlemen to say to these instances? " Cannot they manage to assure us " the prospect is delusive? Hear how " they are characterised. Enclosures " of waste or commons *would* be use- " ful, *if* divided into *small allotments*, " and given up to be occupied at mo- " derate rent by the poor. But *if*, " besides lessening the produce of fine " wool, they bear hard on the poor, " by depriving them of part of " their subsistence, and go towards " the increasing of farms already too

" large,

" large, the advantages attending " them may not much exceed the dif- " advantages *." " Hence," says Mr. Young, " we find all these improve- " ments very *equivocal*. Before it is " allowed that the converting ling to " corn is beneficial, it must be pre- " viously asked, if the improvement " is wrought by that ghostly object " of dread and terror, *a great farmer*; " before it is acknowledged right to " make that sand which would not " feed *rabbits* produce *beef* and *mut-* " *ton*, we must know whether the

* Note, p. 270. Rev. Payments, 4th Edit. printed before.

" poor

" poor were deprived of part of their " subsistence; before you will submit " to change the heaths of Lincoln to " fertile fields of sanfoine, you must " demand, were the *allotments small?* " I must own it is with astonishment " that I thus see superior minds stoop- " ing to prejudices so unworthy of " their abilities ‡."

From

‡ What influence all this, and much more in the same strain, equally pointed and forcible, has had upon the sentiments of Dr. Price, is pretty clear from his re-printing what he had before published, and taking no notice of what had been ad- vanced

From a candid review of the above oppoſite repreſentations and reaſonings, it appeared to me undeniable that Encloſures, according to particular circumſtances, are attended with great advantages and great diſadvantages reſpecting the grand object of enquiry, the encreaſe of our people; but that ſtill it was not abſolutely certain and free from all poſſibility of controverſy, which of the two, in the vaſt number of Encloſures which had taken place in this kingdom, during the laſt 20 or 30 years, had been moſt nume-

---

vanced in anſwer by this experienced and practical writer.

rous

rous and prevalent. Probability, indeed, ſeemed ſtrongly on the favourable ſide. I thought, however, that I ſhould be much more clear in this point, if I could procure the annual regiſters of baptiſms in the pariſhes recently incloſed during the laſt 20 years. If theſe pariſhes, when taken in the aggregate, were not materially *decreaſed*, it would be a ſtrong preſumption that Encloſures had advanced our total Population; (becauſe it was an undoubted fact that in ſome few places, where open cultivated fields had been converted into paſtures, the number of inhabitants on thoſe particular ſpots had been greatly leſſened): If they were actually not at *all diminiſhed*, *nifhed*, but even very much *increafed*, the conclufion would be ftronger ftill; if, finally, they were not only *increafed*, but *increafed* even more than thofe parifhes which had *not* been recently enclofed, it would amount to very little lefs than abfolute demonftration. In purfuit of thefe ideas I immediately procured a lift of the Enclofure-bills, from the Journals of the Houfe of Commons, and found, to my furprize, that they amounted to very near a thoufand, between the year 1750 and 1781. I foon difpatched about about 500 letters to the clergy of the enclofed parifhes, omitting however the counties of Nottingham, York, and

 Lancafter,

Lancaſter, becauſe Dr. Price himſelf acknowledged thoſe to be greatly encreaſed. Of theſe 500 letters I have been favoured with anſwers to hardly a hundred. Small however as this proportion is, yet coming from all quarters indifferently, and without any previous motive for choice or ſelection, their evidence may fairly be conſidered as ſatisfactory and deciſive. What this evidence is the reader may ſee in the following table:

The

[To face p. 26.]

The number of Baptiſms during two periods of five years each, the firſt beginning with 1760, the ſecond with 1775, in a great number of recently encloſed pariſhes, from different counties, together with the Baptiſms in other pariſhes not recently encloſed, in the ſame counties reſpectively.

COUNTIES.	Baptiſms in Pariſhes lately encloſed.			Baptiſms in Pariſhes not lately encloſed.		
	Numb of Pariſhes.	1ſt Period.	2d Period.	Numb. of Pariſhes.	1ſt Period.	2d Period.
Northumberland	2	349	441	32	5977	6302
Durham	3	525	600	10	2735	3202
Cumberland	3	956	1147	20	2431	2823
Shropſhire	3	390	517	17	1729	1782
Norfolk	8	447	558	69	4384	5224
Eſſex	2	165	248	19	1517	1920
Bedford	3	151	221	6	981	935
Bucks	4	343	335	8	1490	1748
Leiceſter	7	1255	1450	8	1021	1340
Stafford	2	320	356	10	2394	2860
Warwick	12	1269	1609	7	1154	1446
Derby and Berks	5	546	621	25	2135	2413
Middleſex	1	34	47	4	827	1073
Worceſter	7	1490	1946	17	2011	2493
Glouceſter	10	463	588	175	13163	14639
Wilts	13	1888	2187	48	5774	4210
Hants	4	213	267	15	3008	3374
Totals	89	10804	13138	490	52731	57984
Increaſed nearly as		100 to	121	as	100 to	109

In this Table we ſee that the recently encloſed pariſhes have vaſtly the advantage of thoſe which have not been recently encloſed. The baptiſms in the 89 pariſhes of the former deſcription, during the five years, beginning with the year 1760, to the baptiſms during the five years beginning with 1775, or 1776, are nearly as 100 to 121; whereas in the 490 of the latter, for the ſame periods reſpectively, the advance is only as 100 to 109; that is, the Encloſures are increaſed more than $\frac{1}{5}$th, the non-incloſures ſcarcely $\frac{1}{10}$th. This is ſurely little leſs than abſolute demonſtration of the point in queſtion, the influence of Encloſures upon the Population of this kingdom, and that, ſo far from having diminiſhed, they have much increaſed it. It is alſo to be obſerved, that the increaſe from hence ariſing is certainly greater than here appears; becauſe thoſe Encloſures which converted arable to paſture, muſt have leſſened the employment of the inhabitants, and of courſe their number, in the ſeveral pariſhes in which they reſpectively took place, and proportionably augmented and employed thoſe in pariſhes where Encloſures had *not* taken place. It may be ſaid, perhaps, that the increaſe of the encloſed pariſhes may have been occaſioned by cauſes totally diſtinct from the Encloſures. I make no doubt but that with regard to ſome of them this has really been the caſe; but then it ſhould be remembered, that there is no reaſon to ſuppoſe that the ſame cauſes have not operated likewiſe in the non-encloſed pariſhes, and conſequently that the *difference* of the increaſe, and even *more* than that difference, for the reaſon juſt now aſſigned, muſt have ariſen from the Encloſures alone. Had indeed an Encloſure of only 50 or 60 acres, belonging to ſuch a town as Birmingham, been included in my liſt of encloſed pariſhes, that alone might have turned the balance on the favourable ſide, and nearly deſtroyed the argument; as the prodigious augmentation of people there has doubtleſs been occaſioned by the enormous growth of its manufactures, which, however, the vaſt improvements of agriculture have helped to ſupport and maintain.

maintain. But no ſuch towns are included; I took in merely country pariſhes and market towns of the common ſize and deſcription, as they happened to ariſe. The towns of Sheffield, Mancheſter, Liverpool, &c. I need not ſay are excluded, as I admitted not a ſingle pariſh encloſed or unencloſed, from the counties of either York or Lancaſter.

That Encloſures have increaſed our Population is alſo fairly deducible from the militia returns for the county of Rutland. Mr. J. Bramſton, clerk of the Militia meetings there, has favoured me with the number of men liable to ſerve in every pariſh reſpectively through-

throughout the county, from the year 1759 to 1779, both inclufive.

This county confifts of 56 or 57 parifhes. Of thefe 10 have been enclofed within the laft 25 years, and which, in point of population, feem to comprehend about a fourth part of the whole. Now fuppofing the total number of inhabitants to remain the fame, and the exemptions from this fervice to continue invariable, the returns of men liable to ferve muft, for fome time, perpetually decreafe, as the perfons who have once ferved are excufed for the future. But befides this caufe of diminution, the exemptions from fervice fince the year 1759 have been greatly multiplied. From both causes jointly, the returns for 1779 must be vastly less than that in 1759, unless a prodigious increase of people has taken place. But these causes of decrease have extended uniformly to every part of the county, the recently enclosed parishes as well as the others; consequently, if the Population has been unvaried, the proportion of decrease in the returns must be unvaried likewise. Now the returns of men liable to serve in 1759 in the 47 parishes, which have not been since inclosed, amounted to 1773; the returns for the same in 1779 were 1196, i. e. they were decreased nearly in the proportion of 148 to 100. The returns for the ten parishes inclosed within the

last

laſt 25 years, at the ſame two periods reſpectively, were 557 and 397, which is a decreaſe in the ratio of only 140 to 100, or more than $\frac{1}{10}$th leſs than the others.

The ſame general concluſions, or even more favourable ones, reſult from another view of theſe returns. The exemptions of men liable to ſerve in the year 1769 were the ſame as in the year 1779. The returns in the non-encloſures in 1769 were 1176, in the year 1779, 1146: for the ten Encloſures in 1769, 388, and in 1779, 397; (i. e.) the returns of the former were actually *decreaſed* almoſt one-fortieth part, and the returns of the latter nearly as much *increased* *.

Upon

* This, applied to the whole county, indicates a considerable increase of people. The total return of men liable to serve in 1769 was 1564, in 1779, 1543; a diminution of only 21. But in the interval of time now referred to, there had been three successive returns, at each of which additional exemptions took place, equal in number to the whole body of the county Militia (i. e.) 120; amounting in the whole to 360 men. It is likewise to be observed, that before the last return, it being the very height of the American war, supplies were doubtless furnished from this county both to the Army and Navy, of exactly the same description with the persons liable to serve in the Militia. These considerations duly

attended

Upon the whole, then, the comparative advantage of Enclosures for the

---

attended to, it is extremely manifest that the number of men really fit for military service, must, at the last return, after every fair allowance and deduction made, have been increased between three and four hundred; which implies an increased Population of at least 12 or 16 hundred in the course of 10 years.

The number of houses returned to the Tax-office for the county of Rutland in the year 1777 was only 1474, and consequently, according to Dr. Price's mode of computation, it contained very few more than 7000 inhabitants; whereas, from the Militia returns, and other data, they cannot be so little as 12,000.

encreaſe of Population ſeems indubitably clear, from a moſt ſtriking concurrence of a great variety of evidence. It appears from the reaſon and nature of the thing, from the teſtimony of very extenſive obſervation, from the above Militia returns, and from the regiſters of Baptiſms promiſcuouſly taken in 18 or 20 counties. So far therefore from expreſſing my aſtoniſhment at the folly of our parliament in granting ſuch numerous bills of Encloſure, I only wiſh it may go on granting ſtill more, under due regulations and reſtrictions, till there is ſcarcely an uninloſed or waſte and barren ſpot from one extremity of the kingdom to the other, but

all

all are converted into fruitful fields, or luxuriant paſtures, and the whole reſembles one large, rich and variegated garden.

F I N I S.

A P P E N D I X.

THE following letter, which I was favoured with by the Reverend Mr. Woodhouſe, of Donington, in Shropſhire, is not, all of it, indeed, to the immediate purpoſe of the preceding enquiry; much of it, however, certainly is, and the whole of it is written with ſo much good ſenſe and ingenuity, and affords ſo ſtrong a preſumption of an increaſed population in country pariſhes, where agriculture has been improved, that I cannot content myſelf with the ſuppreſſion of any part of it.

'Donington, near Shifnal, Shropſhire,
'June 8, 1782.

'Rev. Sir,

'I have been as expeditious as poſſible 'in numbering the inhabitants of this pa'riſh, and with pleaſure tranſmit to you 'the following particulars:

'About the year 1689, the Reverend 'George Plaſton, then Rector of 'the pariſh, took the number of his 'pariſhioners, which appears to 'have been - - - -	138
'In 1777, upon my entrance into 'the pariſh, I numbered the inha'bitants, to the amount of - -	232
'In 1782, I have done the ſame at 'your requeſt, and the number ap'pears to be - - - -	263

'The

'The increase of the inhabitants since
'the Revolution has therefore been very
'great; it has also been very regular, as
'may be collected from the whole of our
'Parochial Register, but will appear suffi-
'ciently from the following extracts, which
'you have particularly desired:

20 years, from 1688.	Baptisms	55
	Marriages	23
	Burials	41
20 years, from 1730.	Baptisms	104
	Marriages	23
	Burials	61
20 years, from 1760.	Baptisms	133
	Marriages	36
	Burials	79

'So considerable and regular an increase
'in the number of inhabitants cannot be
'ascribed to accident, but must be imputed
'to some permanent cause, continually ope-
'rating.

'Commerce and manufactures are acknowledged causes of a regular population, but I cannot find that any commerce, trade, or manufacture has ever been carried on in this parish. The inhabitants have seldom made their own shoes. Husbandry has been their only occupation, and has been transmitted from father to son, with such improvements as have justly established it an adequate cause of the great increase of our people. For,

'1st. The tradition and testimony of the inhabitants informs us, that a considerable part of the parish, now in cultivation, was formerly over-grown with underwood, broom, furze, &c. and consequently employed very few hands, and returned very little profit to its occupier; as land became more valuable, (and why more valuable, but because the surrounding country became more populous) the owners were tempted to make it fit for the plough, and to put it into a course of

'tillage,

'tillage, which could not be effected with-'
'out an increaſe of labour. Employment
'produced induſtry, induſtry good wages;
'theſe encouraged the labourers to marry
'early, and to produce children, who ſoon
'entered upon employment, maintained
'themſelves, married; and thus our Regiſter
'of baptiſms has been ſwelled ſo conſider-
'ably beyond that of burials, accounting
'for that regular increaſe of inhabitants,
'which appears upon every ſurvey.

'2. Not only the wider extent, but in an'
'equal, or, perhaps, greater, degree, the
'improved method of cultivation, provid-
'ing an additional employment for the
'inhabitants, has conſequently increaſed
'their number. The land which uſed to be'
'ſowed at one ploughing, and then be left'
'wholly to the mercy of the ſeaſon, is now
'diligently tilled, and kept clean from
'weeds by the hand and the hoe. A gar-
'den requires more labour than a field of
'equal ſize; and in proportion as we ſtudy
"more

'more and more to make every field neat 'and productive as a garden, we encou- 'rage and increase the number of our in- 'habitants. The introduction of the turnip- 'husbandry into this parish, about twenty 'years ago, has certainly added not only to 'the richness and frequency of the crops, 'but also to the number of the people.

'3. If the increase of the inhabitants 'has of late been more rapid than ordinary, 'it is justly to be attributed to the *enclosure* 'which took place in this parish about 'twelve years ago. The field-land, which 'lay open, and could only be tilled after a 'certain old fashioned course, is now im- 'proved as the proprietor pleases; and, 'being generally cultivated after the alter- 'nating course used in Norfolk, where 'turnips well hoed are the certain fore- 'runners of other profitable crops, increases 'the labour, and consequently the popula- 'tion of the parish. But our numbers are 'affected in a still more visible manner by

'the

'the *enclosure of the common*, which then
'bore little, and bad grass, but now pro-
'duces turnips, clover, and grain, and
'cannot be managed without an increase
'of labour and hands. Accordingly, we
'find four houses erected since the enclo-
'sure of the common, containing an addi-
'tional tenth to the whole number of
'inhabitants; for before the enclosure the
'number of houses was forty-one, now it is
'forty-five.

'Thus, Sir, am I able to present you
'with the returns of a parish whose popu-
'lation, has been almost doubled since the
'time of the Revolution, yet, whose in-
'crease of inhabitants can only be ascribed
'to such causes, as must have operated in
'a similar manner in most other parishes of
'Great Britain. And lest any person should
'suppose that our increase of inhabitants
'has been effected by a decrease in other
'parishes, I bring my Register to witness,
'that in the whole period of time, from
'the

'the Revolution to the present hour, 54
'persons have been born over and above
'those that can be accounted for, either in
'the burials, or present increased number of
'inhabitants.

'Baptisms since 1688 - - - -	442
'Accounted for in the burials -	263
'In the increased number of inhabi-'tants - - - - - -	125
	388
'Remain unaccounted for in our own 'parish, and consequently must have 'migrated to other parishes - -	54
	442

'Hence it appears that this parish has not
'received its increase from other parishes,
'but has contributed to their population.
'And it deserves likewise to be considered,
'that as the inhabitants of Donington are
'all husbandmen, and do not manufacture
'their own clothes, furniture, tools, uten-
sils,

'fils, &c. so, as they increase in population and riches, they require and employ more tradesmen in the neighbouring towns and villages to supply them with the necessaries, comforts, and, indeed, luxuries of life: — consequently, here is an increase of population in other parishes occasioned by our increase; and not only in this respect, but in another, which is by no means insignificant. For as we continue to raise more and more grain for the mill, meat for the shambles, wool for the clothier, &c. &c. it is evident that we find employment for, and increase the number of those who grind and retail the corn, make and sell the malt, retail the meat, manufacture the wool, &c. and that the number of consumers must be likewise proportionably increased.

'Thus population is the necessary consequence of an improved agriculture; of which I have been able, as I hope, to 'afford you a convincing ſpecimen. If I 'have erred in any of my deductions, I 'beg you will correct me, and that you 'will apply what I now tranſmit to you, 'in whatever ſhape or manner you find 'moſt uſeful or convenient to your very 'laudable deſign. I have the pleaſure to 'ſubſcribe myſelf, with all the reſpect that 'is due to your beneficent undertakings,

'Reverend Sir,

'Your truly humble ſervant,

'J. CHAPPEL WOODHOUSE,

'Rector of Donington.'

I need make no apology to the reader for preſenting him with this letter. Whoever has the ſame conception of its excellence which I have, will rather be inclined to reproach me for having ſo long deprived him of the pleaſure of peruſing it. It is, in my apprehenſion, one of the beſt Eſſays, if if I may properly give it that appellation, I ever read upon the ſubject, either in print or manuſcript. The reaſoning is every where clear and perſpicuous, the illuſtrations peculiarly happy, and the concluſions juſt and deciſive.

I intended here to have ſubjoined an Examination of a Pamplet intitled, *A political Enquiry into the Conſequences of encloſing Waſte Lands, and the Cauſes of the preſent high Price of Butcher's Meat, being the Sentiments of a Society of Farmers in ——ſhire*. But I ſoon found that a full diſcuſſion of only its leading arguments, and a ſatisfactory detection of the numerous defects and fallacies with which they abound, would carry me to a very conſiderable length. And I could by no means ſatisfy myſelf with a few ſuperficial remarks upon a work which, in my apprehenſion, contains many pernicious aſſertions, enforced by no inconſiderable degree of ingenuity and eloquence. I

therefore

therefore reſerved my Examination of it, as the buſineſs of a ſeparate Pamphlet, which, it being already nearly finiſhed, ſhall ſoon appear. I was the rather induced to this meaſure, as *the Political Enquiry*, &c. the immediate ſubject of the propoſed inveſtigation, ſeems to have received a very advantageous character from perſons, the rectitude of whoſe general deciſions is entitled to reſpectful deference, and who have no inconſiderable influence in forming the judgement of the publick.

FINIS.

ENCLOSURES,

A Cause of improved Agriculture, of Plenty and Cheapness of Provisions, of Population, and of both private and national Wealth;

BEING

An EXAMINATION of two PAMPHLETS, entitled,

THE ONE,

A Political Enquiry into the Consequences of enclosing Waste Lands, and the Cause of the present high Price of Butcher's Meat, &c.

THE OTHER,

Cursory Remarks upon Enclosures, by a Country Farmer;

TOGETHER WITH

Some slight OBSERVATIONS upon the

REPORT OF THE LONDON COMMITTEE,

Appointed the 16th of July, 1786, to consider the Causes of the present high Prices of Provisions.

By the Rev. J. HOWLETT,
Vicar of Great Dunmow, Essex.

———— ————The Waste shall smile
With yellow Harvests; what was barren Heath
Shall soon be verdant Mead.

MASON'S GARDEN, B. I. l. 109.

Enclosing would not be encouraged if Provisions were not at a high Price, and the Practice must soon cease when it becomes so disadvantageous as it would be if it tended to depopulate.

CRIT. REV. 1786. p. 393.

LONDON:
PRINTED FOR W. RICHARDSON, ROYAL EXCHANGE,
M DCC LXXXVII.

Republished in 1973 by Gregg International Publishers Limited
Westmead, Farnborough, Hants, England

ADVERTISEMENT.

AGREEABLY to what I intimated in the Appendix to my *Enquiry into the Influence of Enclosures upon the Population of this Kingdom*, the greater part of the following pamphlet was ready for the press six months ago; but, upon the suggestion of an obliging correspondent, I was induced to wait for still further intelligence. This intelligence, at my request, has since been furnished by the following gentlemen: Mr. Thomas Davis, of Longleat, Somerset, Steward to Lord Weymouth; John Billingsley, Esq. of Ashwick; Benjamin Pryce, Esq. of Sarum; Thomas Tyley, Esq. agent to the Duke of Chandos in Somersetshire; Mr. Thomas Fricker, of Deverell Longbridge, Wilts, a sensible farmer of fifty years experience; and many other skilful farmers and graziers in South Wales, as well as in the southern, western, and midland counties of England. Of these persons, some have long been eminently distinguished for their agricultural knowledge in general, others for their extensive observation and great experience

perience respecting enclosures in particular. Their several communications are inserted in the following pages. In most instances they afford the confirmation of fact to what I had previously advanced on my own judgment: in others they contain sentiments, or suggest hints, of considerable importance. For both the former and the latter I think myself greatly obliged to them; and they will, I hope, excuse the liberty I take of thus publicly returning my thanks.

CONTENTS.

SECTION III.

This

SECTION IV.

SECTION V.

Miscellaneous Objections considered.

2. *Objections*

ERRATA.

P. ii. l. 2 from the bottom, for *his* read *its*. P. iii. l. 3, for *his* read *this*. P. 19, l. 8, for 1748, read 1740. P. 35, Note, l. 6, between *kept* and *in* insert *upon*. P. 48, l. 7, for 1739 read 1739-40: l. 9, for *forty following ones*, read *following one*. P. 74, l. 2, for *as plants* read *and plants*. P. 77, l. 9, for *or any*, read *upon any*. P. 79, l. 2, for *her* read *their*. P. 91, l. 8, dele *and*,

INTRODUCTION, &c.

IN the preſent ſtate of ſociety in Europe, an increaſe of people is, generally ſpeaking, of all others, the moſt unequivocal proof of an increaſe of proſperity. Having, therefore, in my enquiry concerning the influence of encloſures upon the population of this kingdom, proved, I think, nearly to demonſtration, (a) that they have not only augmented our numbers, but even more augmented them than any other cauſe in ſimilar ſituations, I judged all further evidence of their utility utterly ſuperfluous. The fact, that they have already produced this conſequence, being once eſtabliſhed, every argument againſt the practice, whether deduced from ſpeculative reaſoning, or

(a) The method I took for aſcertaining this, ſeemed to me the only practicable one; and had my enquiries been anſwered to their full extent, the demonſtration would have been complete.

Mr. Stone, indeed, in a late valuable publication, has made ſome objections, which I am perſuaded he would not have made, if he had duly attended to the nature and limitation of my argument. I ſhall only here obſerve, that his objections are, in ſome meaſure, totally groundleſs; but as far as they are really founded, they only ſtrengthen and confirm my general concluſions.

general obſervation, however plauſible on a general view, we may be certain is ſomewhere or other defective and fallacious.

The matter however appears to others, it ſeems, in a very different light. The Monthly Reviewers, whoſe judgment in general deſerves reſpect, in their Review for May laſt, have, as it were, recommended to my peruſal an anonymous pamphlet, entitled, *A Political Enquiry into the Conſequences of encloſing Waſte Lands, and the Cauſes of the preſent High Price of Butchers Meat, being the Sentiments of a Society of Farmers in ——ſhire,* and have obſerved upon it, that the objections of this writer ſtill remain in their full force. Upon a recommendation ſo truly reſpectable, and finding likewiſe that the work had had conſiderable influence in different parts of the kingdom, I immediately procured it, and have read it through with all the attention the importance of the ſubject demands. The reſult is, that I think it contains, as far as the main purpoſe is concerned, many ſentiments ſo extremely falſe, and of ſuch pernicious tendency, that they ought not to paſs without a full refutation, eſpecially as they are enforced with a vivacity of remark, and urged with a copiouſneſs of language, highly plauſible and impoſing.

There is no probability, indeed, that his reaſonings will have any influence on the meaſures of government.

govenrment. Commiſſioners have been appointed to enquire into the ſtate of the *crown and foreſt lands* ſince the publication of his pamphlet, and there is little doubt but that ſuch of them will be encloſed, as, upon fair examination, appear capable of due improvement. But every good citizen will not only rejoice in the ſalutary regulations of the ſtate to which he belongs, but alſo wiſh to remove from the minds of others ſuch groundleſs diſcontent as the publication before us, from the plauſible air it aſſumes, is extremely well fitted to infuſe.

The author has ſo dreadful an idea of *encloſures*, that " he apprehends the univerſal cul-" tivation of the waſte lands in Great-Britain, " would be ſo far from a benefit, that it would " be the greateſt evil to this country that could " poſſibly befall it, except that of being abſolutely " ſwallowed up, and ſunk in the bowels of the " ocean." This extravagant aſſertion he endeavours to enforce by the following illuſtration. " If " a beggar comes to me for relief from hunger, " and I give him half a quartern loaf for nothing, " no perſon will pretend to aſſert that if he had " bought a whole loaf at the baker's, and given " ſeven-pence halfpenny for it, that becauſe he " would in that caſe have had a greater plenty, " that therefore it was cheaper than my half loaf

" was. And this is nearly the caſe with regard to " the cattle now fed on commons; the little they " get is not paid for, and therefore the owners can " afford to ſell them cheaper than if they paid for " their food, either by the way of rent of land, " or any other means." To this I ſhall only reply at preſent, that if the ſame beggar came to me, and I enabled him, in conſequence of encloſing my waſtes and commons, to earn, by induſtrious labour, what would purchaſe *two loaves*, whoever will not allow I do *him*, as well as the community, a greater and more eſſential ſervice than if I had given him *half a loaf for nothing*, I have only to wiſh, for his full conviction, that he would take up his reſidence in a land of beggars, ſurrounded with lazineſs and indolence, and all their miſerable diſguſtful attendants.

Our author's bold aſſertion, however, *that the univerſal cultivation of our waſtes, &c. would be the greateſt calamity that could befall us, next to being ſwallowed up, and ſunk in the bowels of the ocean*, notwithſtanding its ſtartling ſound, is a mere harmleſs hyperbole, meaning nothing more, in plain Engliſh, than that *beef and mutton would be advanced to ninepence or a ſhilling a pound.* For this appears the ultimate object he has all along in view, the grand point he directs all his arguments to eſtabliſh.

In order to accomplish this purpose, he lays down, as fundamental maxims, a few self-evident propositions, and then institutes upon them a course of the most fallacious and inconclusive reasoning that can be conceived.

" Even gold," says he, " may be bouhgt too " dear, and so may corn and grass, or any other " of the useful productions of nature." Undoubtedly. " *Plenty* of the necessaries of life, " abstractedly considered, is not of so much be- " nefit to a nation as most people are apt to think." Probably. " For it is only when that plenty " causes a *cheapness* that enables every rank and " degree of people to purchase a sufficiency for " their subsistance, which constitutes a general be- " nefit to mankind. Granted. " *Plenty* or *scar-* " *city* do not ultimately govern the price of a com- " modity, though it may tend to create a tem- " porary rise or fall to a certain degree." Allowed. " It is *the charge of the production* that stamps the " permanent average price of all kinds of com- " modities whatever. For instance, no possible " plenty of Dutch Holland, or fine muslins of " India, could ever cause these articles to alter for " any length of time to an equal price as the coarse " dowlas; because the manufactory of these fine " articles is so infinitely more expensive than the " coarse." This likewise I have no inclination to dispute. " Admitting then," continues this writer, " that

" that the charge of the production ſtamps the " permanent average price in all kinds of commo- " dities, I may fairly draw this concluſion, that " though by a higher degree of cultivation of the " lands of this country, we might be able to pro- " duce twice as much corn and graſs as we pro- " duce at preſent; yet if that corn and graſs ſo " produced ſhould coſt the nation or the farmer " who produced it, on account of the advanced " rent of lands, and the exorbitant expences in the " cultivation, twice as much per load, as the price " of theſe articles are at preſent, neither the na- " tion nor the farmer would mend their condition; " on the other hand, the poor would ſuffer double " the diſtreſſes they now ſuffer, unleſs their " wages were doubled; and if their wages were " doubled, this would put a ſtop to all manu- " factures carried on at preſent to ſupply foreign " markets."

Theſe concluſions are readily admitted; but their admiſſion entirely depends upon the ſtrange operation of the little word *if*. Change the appli- cation of this wonder-working conjunction, and we draw concluſions directly oppoſite. *If*, by a higher cultivation of the lands of this country, we might be able to produce three times as much corn and graſs as we produce at preſent, and if the corn and graſs ſo produced ſhould not coſt the nation or the farmer above twice more than the preſent

present product costs, both the nation and the farmer would greatly mend their condition: The farmer could afford to sell his produce of every kind considerably cheaper, the landlord might have larger rent, the poor fuller employment, their distresses would be lessened, and this would powerfully encourage our manufactures carried on to supply foreign markets.

It is a maxim of general application, that lands of the highest rent, and those which are most manured and cultivated, though at great expence, are finally the most profitable. The farmer, who gives a pound an acre annual rent, and lays out triple that sum in improvements, often gets more money, and can afford to sell his corn, his grass, his cattle, at a much lower price than another, who gives not even five shillings an acre, and is at small additional cost of any kind whatever; the difference of product being still greater than the difference of rents and other expences.

The illustration of this from particular facts may easily be given. A small parish in the county of Kent, by the increased and higher cultivation of the land, has its quantity of corn, hay, hops, cattle, &c. three times as great as they were forty years ago; and though the rents have been considerably raised, the price of provisions and the expence of culture greatly augmented, yet the farmers,

farmers, who used to be continually breaking, are now every day growing rich, the number of inhabitants is doubled, the poor, from the advantage of full employment, are in a much more comfortable condition than any I have ever seen upon the borders of a common.

Upon Mendipp Hills in Somersetshire, five thousand *(b)* acres have been enclosed within the same

(b) The detail is as follows:

☞ Names of the enclosures.	No. of Acres.		Average Improvement. s.		s.
Charter House - -	400		4		12
Ashwick - - - - -	200		4		18
Cranmore E. and W.	400		3		12
Ubly - - - - - - -	900		4		16
Haydon - - - - -	300	from	3	per Acre to	12
Doubting and Stoke -	700		3		14
Emborough - - -	600		3		12
Shepton Mallet - -	800		3		15
Blagdon - - - - -	900		not quite compleated.		

Cultivation, expences, and produce of six Acres, enclosed in 1780.

DEBTOR.			£.	s.	d.	CREDITOR.	£. s. d.
1780	Oct.	To 1st plowing 16 per Acre	4	16	0		
1781	March.	Cross Do. - - 12 - - - -	3	12	0		
	May.	To dragging - 8 - - - -	2	8	0		
		20 qs. or 160 bushs. lime per Ac. at 20d. per qr.	10	0	0		
	June.	Spreading lime, &c. - - -	0	18	0		
		Plowing - - - - - - - - -	1	4	0		
		Harrowing - - - - - - - -	0	8	0		
	Sept.	Plowing and sowing - - -	1	16	0	Sacks. By 30 - - - - Wheat at 28s.	42 0
		12 Bush. seed wheat - - -	4	10	0		
1782	Aug.	Reaping and securing - - -	3	0	0		
			32	12	0		
		Balance profit	9	8	0		

In

ſame period. The average improvement in the value of the whole is from about 3s. 6d. to nearly 14s. an acre; and although upon ſome parts of it the expences of tillage, manure, &c. the very firſt year of the encloſure, have been more than five guineas an acre, yet has the immediately ſucceeding crop paid it all, with a ſurplus of about 32 ſhillings an acre, for the rent, &c. While continuing under the plough the bare ſtraw ſupports more cow-cattle during the winter, than the product of the whole year ever maintained prior to the encloſure. And where, in the courſe of a few years it has been laid down with clover, rye-graſs, or other artificial herbage, it keeps four times as many cattle, of almoſt every kind, as it ever did before; and when broken up a ſecond time, by a judicious courſe of management, and without the aſſiſtance of *purchaſed* manure, it appears again with its wonted fertility, producing crops equal to thoſe it yielded when newly encloſed and cultivated.

Here, from the higher cultivation of our lands the farmer is indeed at higher expence, and pays

" In this caſe it appears that there remains a profit of more " than 30s. an acre, which will amply repay the expence of " encloſing, and if the land be valued in its *unencloſed* ſtate, at " 4s. an acre, and in its improved one only at 12s. there is, " as it were, a kind of new creation of two thirds more land, " or at leaſt property improved equivalent thereto.——Hear " this, ye enemies of encloſures, and bluſh !"

his landlord a higher rent; yet his products of corn, of grafs, and of cattle, are fo much higher ftill, that after defraying all his extraordinary charges, he has a nett profit of almoft a pound an acre as the reward of his labour and induftry. Is not then the farmer enriched; is not the landlord enriched, are not the poor more fully employed, and, if it be not their own fault, their diftreffes greatly leffened? Are not all thefe a national benefit? Is not this abundance, thus amply paying the expence which attended the production, the fureft ground for cheapnefs of provifions? And muft not this powerfully tend to encourage our manufactures carried on to fupply foreign markets?

Thefe general remarks, and thefe general reafonings, thus fupported by facts, may be confidered, it is prefumed, as a fufficient anfwer to the general remarks and general reafonings of our author, which have no other ground than mere fpeculation. I will now proceed to a particular examination of his great and leading pofitions, which are,

1ft, That the enclofures which have taken place in the courfe of the laft 30 years, have already advanced the price of butcher's meat three (c) halfpence

(c) Our author afferts, indeed, that the price of butcher's meat is advanced even *two-pence* in the lb. more than the advance

halfpence in the pound more than the advance of price in other things.

2d, That ſhould all the waſte lands in the kingdom be encloſed and cultivated, the price of butcher's meat would be raiſed to nine-pence or a ſhilling in the pound.

Theſe are the grand points his whole book is intended to eſtabliſh; and, in anſwer to them, I will endeavour to ſhew,

1, That the aſſertion that the price of butcher's meat is advanced three halfpence in the pound, in the courſe of the laſt thirty years, more than the advance of price in other things, is not true.

2, Granting it to be true, that our encloſures cannot have occaſioned it.

3, Allowing even both, that there is not the ſmalleſt probability that the encloſure and cultivation of all our waſtes and commons would raiſe the price of

advance in other articles; but one halfpenny of this he aſcribes to the encreaſed number of horſes; which, if his computation might be depended upon, would be the moſt plauſible concluſion he has made. He ſays, p. 87, &c. that we now maintain eight hundred thouſand horſes more than we did fifty years ago; which muſt imply, on the moſt moderate allowance, an annual conſumption of at leaſt ten millions worth of corn, graſs, and hay.

butcher's meat to nine pence or a ſhilling in the pound. And,

4, Admitting all the three facts, that ſtill our author's arguments againſt encloſures would be inconcluſive.

Theſe four propoſitions I will endeavour to prove, and I requeſt the reader's cloſe and candid attention through the whole attempt, neither expecting nor deſiring they may further obtain his aſſent, than they are founded in reaſon and truth.

S F. C-

SECTION I.

The Assertion that the Price of Butcher's Meat is advanced three Halfpence in the Pound more than the Advance of Price in other Things, is not true.

THIS proposition, indeed, if we may believe our author in the latter part of his pamphlet, he has himself proved for me, however inconsistent it may be with some of his general maxims, and though entirely subversive of his leading purpose. He says, p. 101, that, "daily "experience verifies that one article of provision "advancing in price, makes the rest of the "articles rise in nearly the same proportion." If this be true, what becomes of the assertion that the price of butcher's meat is advanced three halfpence in the pound more than that of other things? What is it but asserting what he assures us daily experience contradicts?

I wish not, however, to avail myself of apparent inconsistencies. I leave them to produce their natural effect in the mind of the reader. My present business is to prove that the assertion "that "butcher's meat has advanced in price during "the last thirty years three halfpence in the pound "more

" more than the advance of price in other things," *is not true.*

To establish this point it would be extremely trifling to give the result of my own very confined observations. The price of provisions in any particular county, in any particular part of a county, or at any particular market, could not be considered as the standard for the kingdom at large. In this extensive view, the only one that concerns the present inquiry, the most satisfactory evidence, with respect to pork, beef, butter, cheese, &c. is to be sought at the victualling office; and with regard to wheat, barley, &c. in the corn registers; and this not for a single year, but from the average of several years in immediate succession.

As to the former of the abovementioned articles, the testimony of the Victualling Office may be seen in the following tables.

Prices

Prices of Beef and Pork, at the Victualling Office, extracted from Mr. A. Young's Political Arithmetic, p. 141, 2.

Years.	Beef per Cwt.		Pork per Cwt.	
	s.	*d.*	*s.*	*d.*
1740	23	$7\frac{3}{4}$	31	$0\frac{1}{2}$
1741	24	$9\frac{1}{2}$	36	$3\frac{1}{4}$
1742	24	4	32	9
1743	19	$2\frac{1}{2}$	27	$2\frac{1}{4}$
1744	18	$3\frac{1}{2}$	22	$5\frac{1}{4}$
1745	19	$9\frac{1}{2}$	21	$9\frac{1}{4}$
1746	21	$3\frac{3}{8}$	24	$8\frac{1}{4}$
1747	19	$4\frac{1}{4}$	24	$0\frac{1}{2}$
1767	25	$5\frac{1}{2}$	none bought	
1768	25	$3\frac{1}{2}$	ditto	
1769	22	9	33	0
1770	22	$2\frac{1}{2}$	41	5
1771	22	6	43	$3\frac{1}{2}$

Prices of Beef and Pork at the Victualling Office, as sent me by a Friend there, July 4th, 1786.

Years.	Beef per Cwt. s.	d.	Pork per Cwt. s.	d.
1772	26	3	52	6
1773	24	0	*49	11
1774	*28	8½	38	3
1775	*30	4½	44	7½
1776	*28	7	42	11¾
1777	*28	5⅓	*43	11½
1778	25	8	*43	0
1779	*33	2	38	6
1780	*31	2	*40	9
1781	26	3	37	6
1782	*26	8	41	0
1783	30	0	none purchased	
1784	none purchased		Ditto.	
1785	25 ready money	6	45 ready money	

(1772–1784:) These purchases were paid for by bills in course.

N. B. The Prices mark'd thus (*) are average, the others real.

The

The ſame obliging Friend has ſince ſent me the annual Average Coſt of *Butter* and *Cheeſe* at the Victualling-Office from 1750 to 1786, both incluſive, as under.

Years.	Butter per lb. *d.*	Cheeſe Cheſh. per lb. *d.*	Do. Suffolk per lb. *d.*
1750	5		$1\frac{5}{16}$
1751	$4\frac{1}{4}$		$1\frac{1}{4}$
1752	$4\frac{1}{2}$		$1\frac{1}{4}$
1753	4	$2\frac{3}{4}$	$1\frac{1}{4}$
1754	$5\frac{1}{4}$		$1\frac{1}{8}$
1755	$5\frac{3}{8}$		$1\frac{3}{8}$
1756	$5\frac{1}{4}$		$1\frac{1}{4}$
1757	$5\frac{7}{16}$	3	$1\frac{1}{4}$
1758	$5\frac{1}{2}$	$3\frac{1}{4}$	$1\frac{3}{8}$
1759	$5\frac{7}{16}$	3	
1760	$4\frac{1}{2}$	$2\frac{1}{2}$	
Delivered at Plymouth	$4\frac{1}{4}$	$2\frac{1}{2}$	
1761	$5\frac{3}{4}$	$2\frac{1}{2}$	
1762	5	$2\frac{3}{4}$	
1763	$6\frac{3}{8}$	$3\frac{7}{16}$	
1764	$5\frac{3}{8}$	$2\frac{15}{16}$	
1765	$5\frac{3}{4}$	$3\frac{3}{8}$	
1766	$5\frac{1}{16}$	$3\frac{3}{32}$	
1767	$5\frac{3}{8}$	$3\frac{3}{16}$	
1768	$5\frac{1}{2}$	$2\frac{13}{16}$	
1769	$5\frac{9}{16}$	$2\frac{14}{16}$	

Years.	Butter pr. lb.	Cheese Chesh. per lb.	Cheese Suffolk per lb.
	d.	*d.*	
1770	$5\frac{7}{8}$	$3\frac{3}{8}$	
1771	$6\frac{3}{8}$	$3\frac{1}{4}$	
1772	$6\frac{1}{2}$	$3\frac{5}{8}$	
1773	7	$3\frac{3}{4}$	
1774	$6\frac{1}{2}$	$3\frac{5}{16}$	
1775	$5\frac{15}{16}$	$3\frac{1}{4}$	
1776	$6\frac{3}{8}$	$3\frac{3}{8}$	
1777	$7\frac{1}{2}$	$3\frac{1}{4}$	
1778	8	$3\frac{5}{8}$	
1779	$8\frac{1}{8}$	$3\frac{7}{8}$	
1780	$7\frac{3}{8}$	$3\frac{1}{8}$	
1781	5,8412	3,7977	
1782	6,2035	3,7574	
1783	6,4917	4,5541	
1784	7,3405	4,5512	
1785	$6,\frac{45}{112}$	$4\frac{1}{112}$	
1786 *(d)*	$6,\frac{14}{112}$	$3\frac{96}{112}$	

(d) It is true, that the prices given in this and the preceding tables, are probably much lower than they were at the several periods respectively in the London and other particular markets, when the specified articles were bought for private and domestic use. But this forms no objection to the conclusions deduced from them; because no reason can be given why the proportion between them and the other should be different at different periods.

From

From the preceding *Beef* and *Pork* Tables, it appears that the medium Prices of theſe Articles during three Periods, within the Compaſs of the laſt 46 Years have been nearly as follows:

Periods.	Beef p. lb.	Pork p. lb.
	d.	*d.*
8 Years beginning with 1748	$2\frac{1}{2}\ \frac{42}{112}$	$2\frac{3}{4}\ \frac{77}{112}$
5 Years beginning with 1767	$2\frac{1}{2}\ \frac{12}{112}$	$4\ \frac{23}{112}$
5 Years (the laſt bought) ending with 1785.	$2\frac{3}{4}\ \frac{108}{112}$	$4\frac{1}{4}\ \frac{40}{112}$

From the Butter and Cheeſe Tables, their medium Prices appear to have been, during four Periods of five years each, nearly thus:

Periods.	Butter p. lb.	Cheeſe, Cheſh. p. lb.
	d.	*d.*
5 Years beginning with 1750	$4\frac{3}{4}$	$2\frac{3}{4}$ one year
5 Years beginning with 1760	$5\frac{1}{2}$	$2\frac{3}{4}$
5 Years beginning with 1770	$6\frac{1}{2}$	$3\frac{5}{8}$
5 Years beginning with 1780	$6\frac{1}{2}$	4

As to the Advance in the Price of Corn during the laſt forty Years it may be pretty clearly ſeen by the following Tables:

Average Prices of Corn for nineteen Years, from 1746, to 1765, collected from the best authority that can be obtained. (e)

	Wheat.		Barley.		Oats.	
	s	d.	s.	d.	s.	d.
Per Quarter - - -	32	3	17	8	14	0

Average Prices of the same Grains, respectively, for fourteen Years, from 1771 to 1784, extracted from the Corn Register, established by Act of the 10th of George III.

	Wheat.		Barley.		Oats.	
	s.	d.	s.	d.	s.	d.
Per Quarter - - -	45	8	23	8	16	0

It is evident, upon the slightest inspection of these tables, that butcher's meat, instead of being increased in price three halfpence in the pound more than other articles, is actually increased the *least of all.* Beef, we see, has been advanced during the last forty-six years, not even a half-

(e) Our author says, p. 63, that by undoubted vouchers which were laid before parliament a few years since, the average price of corn, during the last twenty years, has been lower than the average price for the last hundred years. I need make no remarks upon this; as whoever understands the subject will immediately see that it is very little to the purpose.

penny

penny per pound, whereas pork has risen almost a penny; butter, in the course of about 36 years, has been raised one penny three farthings, and cheese one penny farthing, and wheat, which we had been given to understand was not advanced at all, is really advanced more than any thing else; being, on an average, almost one-third higher for 14 years ending January 1784, than during 19 years ending with 1765. (f)

The ground-work, therefore, of our author's eloquent declamation, respecting the direful consequences which have resulted from our recent enclosures, vanishes into nothing, and we might here, of course, very safely terminate our researches; it being by no means necessary to investigate the cause of effects which do not exist. Agreeably, however, to my plan, and that I may give the more full and compleat satisfaction, I will next endeavour to shew, that if these effects really did exist, they could not have proceeded from the enclosures which have taken place in this kingdom during the last thirty or forty years.

(f) See an account of the quantities of corn and grain exported from, and imported into England and Scotland for fourteen years from January 1771 to January 1784, sold by W. Brown, corner of Essex-Street, Strand; and R. Turner, No. 13, Cornhill.

SECTION II.

If the Price of Butcher's Meat has really been advanced three Halfpence in the Pound more than other Things during the last 30 or 40 Years, it cannot have been owing to the Enclosures which have taken place within that Compass of Time.

IF enclosures ever tend to increase the price of butcher's meat, it must surely be when they convert pasture to arable. But that even these do not always produce this effect, the case of Mendip Hills, already stated, seems to afford satisfactory proof. The products of corn alone, we have seen, paid the additional expences ; while the straw clover and artificial grasses maintained more than the usual stock of cattle and sheep. By the same kind of husbandry, similar improvements have been made upon nearly 15,000 acres of almost fruitless common fields and comparatively unprofitable sheep downs, in the south western parts of Wiltshire. What shall we say then to those wet unhealthy marsh lands, upon which, from the unwholesomeness of the feed, the sheep by rot, and the beasts by similar disorders, were often in so sickly, infirm a state, and so frequently died, as to render the rights of commonage of very

very little and precarious value; *(a)* but which, by being enclosed and drained, have been made dry, healthy and luxuriant, supporting as many sheep and oxen, and four times as many milch cows as before? What shall we say particularly to the recent enclosures of this kind in Somersetshire? to those of Wedmore, Blackford, Cross, Huntspill, Glastonbury, Westhay, Mark, Wookey; which

(a) I am assured on the testimony of a very sensible farmer on the borders of Sedgmore, in Somersetshire, that this is now actually the case with that very rich, extensive piece of land, containing 20,000 acres. For want of draining, he observes, it is frequently so unwholesome, (especially after a quick spring of grass) that the cattle fed there are liable to be *baned* (exactly in the manner as sheep) and, that so many die, or never perfectly recover, that the loss more than balances the profit derived from the right of common. Another person from the same quarter informs me, "that in dry summers, "indeed, it maintains cows, oxen, horses, sheep, and geese; "but that in wet summers it is *poison* to them all; and that "although, in favourable seasons, it may be worth from 10s. "to 20s. an acre; yet that from the multiplicity of rights, "from its being sometimes overstocked, and at others under-"stocked; from the diseases the cattle contract there, from the "uncertainty of its produce, to which no farmer, nor set of "farmers can accommodate their stock; from the number of "poor bad horses, that are in themselves unnecessary, are sel-"dom used, and would not be kept at all on enclosed lands; "from these several clogs on its value, he has seldom found "that, in valuing an estate in its vicinity, the farmers were "ever willing to allow any rent for it: whereas by draining, "which cannot be effected without enclosure, it would cer-"tainly be worth from 20 to 40s per acre."

have all taken place within the laſt 12 years, and contain more than 10,000 acres? *(b)* While in common, were they not, by the eſtimation of the moſt ſkilful farmers, of comparatively very little value? But now, in conſequence of being drained and properly managed, are they not let at 25s. an acre? The ſurrounding lands, mean time, inſtead of being diminiſhed in value, are they not even improved, and rented conſiderably higher? Are not the ſheep on moſt of theſe new encloſures, more numerous, and, in the room of being, as formerly, poor and miſerable, and often dying with the rot, are they not even during the winter months, fatted, and made fit for the butcher? Are not the neat cattle, of every kind, more than doubled? Are not the milch cows, in the ſingle pariſh of Wedmore increaſed upwards of 500? And

(b) The detail of the above was furniſhed, at my requeſt, by Mr. Thomas Tyley, of Wedmore, agent to the duke of Chandos in Somerſet. The number of acres in each of the ſpecified incloſures, and the periods at which they reſpectively took place, are as follows:

Dates.	Names.	Acres.
1774	Wedmore	2600
1781	Do. Blackford Manor	950
1778	Croſs	300
1778	Huntſpill	1100
1778	Glaſtonbury	1400
1778	Weſthay	1700
1781	Mark	2000
1783	Wookey	900
		10,950

are

are not theſe, on the moſt moderate allowance, equal to an additional rental of 2000l. a year, excluſive of the number of perſons maintained by the employment they afford ? The horſes too, although not multiplied in number, are they not, from the improvement in the breed, greatly augmented in aggregate value ? The poor, at the ſame time, have been conſtantly ſo much better employed, that the rates have continued nearly the ſame, and do not increaſe, though it is well known that in many other parts of the kingdom, they have been nearly doubled within the period juſt now mentioned. Amidſt this profuſion of produce, theſe multiplied flocks of fattened ſheep, theſe crouded droves of kine and oxen, where is the evidence that theſe encloſures have contributed to heighten the price of beef and mutton ? Would they be ſold the dearer becauſe three times the quantity was ſent to market ? Where is the probability that they could not be afforded as cheap as before ? Or that the increaſed products were not more than equivalent to the increaſed expences ? The improved condition of every rank of people here ſpeaks the contrary.

If neither thoſe encloſures which have left the grounds paſture which were paſture before, nor even thoſe which have converted paſture into tillage, appear to have raiſed the price of butcher's meat, what may we expect from thoſe which have changed tillage into paſture? From thoſe immenſe tracts, for example, in the Vale of Eveſham, in the counties of Worceſter and Glouceſter, which of cold wet and almoſt barren arable, are become dry healthy rich meadow, and, in lieu of ſcanty crops of wheat or barley, are covered with multitudes of fat ſheep and oxen? Nay, what may we expect from thoſe "newly-encloſed lordſhips "in Northamptonſhire and Leiceſterſhire, where," as Dr. Price and Mr. Addington heavily complain, "there are now not 50 acres ploughed yearly where "there uſed to be 1500, and ſcarce an ear of corn "to be ſeen where formerly were grown hundreds "of quarters?" While theſe encloſures, in the fancies of theſe two gentlemen, appear to have raiſed the price of wheat *three ſhillings* in the buſhel, have they, at the ſame time, alſo advanced that of beef and mutton *three halfpence* in the pound? If they have produced effects ſo directly oppoſite, farewell to the dictates of common ſenſe!

As from the inſtances now adduced there ſeems to ariſe a very powerful evidence that the *particular* encloſures referred to have not increaſed the price of butcher's meat, the following facts are a ſtrong preſumption that encloſures in *general* cannot have done it. The average price of beef at the Victualhing Office during the laſt ſeventeen years of the laſt century was about 2¼d. a pound, the four years beginning with 1709 nearly 3¼d. whereas the five years ending with 1771 it was

only

only 2½d. At the *two first* of these periods, none of the recent enclosures, now so severely condemned, had been made; at the *last*, more than half the present number had actually taken place.

All this reasoning, it may be said, however plausible, is so far from being a full refutation of our author's system, that it does not even directly encounter his arguments. For has he not proved, even to demonstration, by a clear and minute detail of particulars, that while *wastes* and *uninclosed commons* remain, the cottager can afford to sell that lean sheep for 10s. which the farmer, on his rich enclosures, cannot bring up for less than 20s. or a guinea? And must there not necessarily be the same difference of price when fatted?

Let me ask in return, can it be possible that his statements and reasonings can be just? If they are, must it not have been the uniform practice of the uninclosed counties, and those abounding with waste lands, to furnish the enclosed ones with lean sheep, and that the enclosed counties can never have afforded to breed for themselves? But how is the fact? Is it not notorious, that the richest and oldest enclosed counties in the kingdom, not only breed a large proportion of their own stock, but regularly furnish their neighbours with theirs? The county of Essex, in which are few wastes, and whoſe encloſures are as highly cultivated as moſt, does ſhe not now, and has ſhe not time immemorial, ſent her lean wethers to be fatted in Hertfordſhire? The counties of Devon and Cornwall, moſt of whoſe waſte lands have been encloſed from the remoteſt antiquity, *(c)* are they not well known to ſupply ſeveral others, eſpecially that of Somerſet, with the greateſt part of their lean ſtock? Do not theſe inſtances give our author's doctrine a doubtful, at leaſt, if not an incredible appearance? For how could theſe things have happened if the wethers in the former caſe, and the ſtock in the latter, could have been purchaſed for half the price upon waſtes and commons? Would it not have recompenſed the grazier to have fetched them from the fartheſt extremities of the iſland? Surely this writer's ſyſtem muſt be unfounded. Let us,

(c) "There are, indeed, ſome conſiderable tracts of un-" incloſed land, a correſpondent remarks, between Exeter and " Holdſworthy, and towards Plymouth; but a great part of " it is not *common*, but private property, and that too worthleſs " to pay for encloſing; and what is really *common*, is ſo exceed-" ingly wet, and boggy, and poor, and ſo much expoſed to the " ſea winds, that were it not for the ſtraw they get from their " encloſures, their cattle could not be ſubſiſted in the winter; " and even with this aſſiſtance it is certain that theſe and the " open grounds of ſimilar kind, whether in Devon or Corn-" wall, do not furniſh their neighbours with half ſo much " ſtock as thoſe parts of either, which have been encloſed " from the earlieſt ages."

however,

however, hear what he has to ſay in ſupport of it.

To eſtabliſh then his favourite and leading point, he gives the following ſtatements of the expences of the farmer and cottager, in the ſituations above repreſented reſpectively.

FARMER's EXPENCES.

Five ewes, producing five wether lambs, coſt keeping the produce of one acre of ground, and for which he pays to his landlord per annum,	1	0	0
On account of pariſh rates, tithes, &c. one fifth more,	0	4	0
Coſt of lambs the firſt year,	1	4	0
Ditto ſecond year,	1	4	0
Ditto third year,	1	4	0
Ditto fourth year,	1	4	0
Groſs coſts of keeping the ſaid five lambs till they become wethers of four years old,	4	16	0
Whence muſt be deducted the profits on the wool, that the five ewes produced the firſt year, and the wool of the five wethers the three ſucceeding years,			

which

	£	s.	d.
Brought over	4	16	0
which I estimate at two todd, viz. half a todd a year, and at 20s. a todd, amounts to	2	0	0
Net costs	2	16	0
Add one fourth of gross cost for loss by rot or accident,	1	4	0
Ditto one-fourth, for profit on labour and attention,	1	4	0
That is about one guinea per head,	5	4	0

COTTAGER's EXPENCES.

	£	s.	d.
Five ewes, producing five wether lambs, kept by a cottager on a common, and boarded at a farm 16 weeks in the winter, at 3d. per head per week,	1	0	0
Expences for boarding the wethers for sixteen weeks, at 2d. per week per head for the second winter,	0	13	4
Ditto for the third winter,	0	13	4
Ditto for the fourth winter,	0	13	4
	3	0	0
" Whence to be deducted, as in the case of the farmer,	2	0	0
Nett cost	1	0	0

Nett

Nett coſt	1	0	0
Add to the nett coſt one fourth of the groſs coſt, for loſs by rot and other accidents,	0	15	0
Ditto for profit on labour,	0	15	0
	2	10	0

" Or ten ſhillings a head.

" That is to ſay, allowing for profits in both " caſes in the ſame proportion, according to pro- " perty riſqued, the farmer's wethers at four *(d)* " years old would ſtand him in one guinea a-piece, " and the cottager's only ten ſhillings."

Theſe are our author's plauſible ſtatements, whence all his wonderful deductions are made.

(d) Our author ſays, that if all our wethers were killed at two years old, the farmer's expences would not, indeed, be ſo much greater than the cottager's, as they are when kept to four years old; but that the produce of wool in the whole kingdom would be diminiſhed one third. This is ſo far from being true, that it would be rather thereby increaſed. For I may venture to appeal to any *Farmer*, or *Society of Farmers*, who know any thing of the matter, that wethers, which have been well kept, at the firſt ſhearing, when a year and four or five months old, produce more wool, in proportion to their *weight*, than ever after. Conſequently, while the conſumption of mutton remains the ſame, the quantity of wool muſt be increaſed by the wethers being all killed at two years old; and the keeping them to four is a mere matter of perſonal luxury, and not of national benefit.

But

But they are every where, and in almoſt every particular, unleſs I am ſtrangely miſtaken, full of deception and fallacy. Sheep of the ſame kind and ſize, as far as appears, are repreſented as kept upon barren commons, as upon fine encloſures of 20s. an acre; their plight, their product of lambs and wool, their riſques and hazards, the expences of labour and attention are alſo given as in equal proportion; whereas nothing, in every reſpect, can be more oppoſite to the truth. But let us examine the two accounts diſtinctly and minutely. And firſt, that of the farmer's

EXPENCES, &c.

This begins with a ſtriking impropriety. The farmer keeps *lean ſheep* three or four years in ſucceſſion upon rich lands of 20s. an acre. A prudent ſkilful man, if upon ſuch land he kept ſheep at all, it would be with a purpoſe and with profits very different from thoſe here ſtated.

An acre of ground of this deſcription, would perhaps ſcarcely be adequate to the maintenance of five Wiltſhire, Hertfordſhire, or Eſſex ſheep. I will ſet them only at four. The reſult in general would be nearly as follows. The four ewes would produce five lambs; two of theſe at leaſt would, in the courſe of the ſummer, be fit for the butcher, making

making from 16s. to a guinea a-piece. The remainder would be worth 12s. each in the month of October or November. Supposing them wethers, they may then be soon put to turnips, or other fattening food, during the winter; and in the ensuing summer, to rye-grass, clover, and the best pasturage the season affords; they will each produce five or six pounds of wool a fleece; and by the Christmas following, having been always so highly fed, will have acquired nearly their full growth, will be sufficiently fat, and worth upon an average 30s. a head. With such mutton as this, a nobleman's house in this neighbourhood used to be constantly supplied, and it was generally allowed to be as good, or the very best that could be procured.

An instance of profit, indeed, much superior to the above, came within my own immediate observation. Five Norfolk ewes were bought some time after Michaelmas 1783, for 16s. a head, and were kept in enclosed fields and pastures of much inferior quality to the above. Early in the spring, 1784, they produced seven lambs, which were all sold to the butcher in the month of May, for 16s. a head. They shore in the summer about half a todd of wool, which was sold for nine-pence per pound. The five sheep took the ram again, and, in the month of August, in the same year, had seven lambs more, which, not long after Michaelmas, made ten ſhillings each. Of the five ewes four, being tolerable meat, were ſold at their original price, in the month of October, and the fifth, early in the next ſpring, fetched a pound. The total produce of theſe five ſheep, in ſomething more than the compaſs of a year, was 9l. 16s. 6d. and all this upon little more than an acre of ground, ſo copious and abundant was the crop of clover. What could unencloſed waſtes and commons have done comparable to either of theſe caſes?

As to the former, few heaths would have kept the Eſſex and the Hertfordſhire ſheep very remote from ſtarving; and as to the fattening the lambs, that would have been quite out of the queſtion. The four ewes would not have reared above four, perhaps only three lambs, which might have fetched about 6 or 8 ſhillings a head, while the wool would not have exceeded 3lb. a fleece, inſtead of 4 or 5. The profits of Norfolk ſheep would perhaps be the moſt certain, as from their manner of bringing up, they are much better ſuited to the rambling vagabond kind of life; they would yield about 2lb. of wool a fleece, and bring four *(e)* lambs, which at Michaelmas might be worth 6 or 7s. a head; ſo that their annual produce might be about

(e) I find from a very excellent account of the expences and profits of a flock of Norfolk ſheep, conſiſting of about 1000, given by the Duke of Grafton, in the 37th No. of Mr. Young's Annals of Agriculture, that on an average of ſeven years, the produce

about 35s. inſtead of 9l. 16s. 6d. as in the inſtance of the encloſures. Whoever will take the pains to compare theſe accounts will find that the farmer could have afforded, after paying rent and other expences, together with the allowance of conſiderable profit, to have *given away his ſecond birth of lambs* as well as the cottager could have afforded his at ſix or ſeven ſhillings a head.

The inſtance indeed of the Norfolk ewes, as firſt above given, is a very extraordinary one, and muſt not be ſtrenuouſly inſiſted on in the preſent argument. But that of the Hertfordſhire, Eſſex, and Wiltſhire is by no means unuſual. The annual produce of four of them we find is upwards of

produce of lambs was ſcarcely four to every five ewes, and of wool about 2lb. a fleece, though they were doubtleſs much better fed and better managed than they uſually are upon waſtes and commons. The average rent of the land too was about 3 or 4s. an acre; and not higher rented than that ſhould our author, perhaps, have ſuppoſed his lean ſheep kept in encloſures.

It ſeems that theſe ſheep are vaſtly more prolific when brought to our rich Eſſex paſtures than when fed upon the poor thin lands of Norfolk. Inſtead of five producing only four lambs, it more commonly happens that four produce five; nay very often a proportion much higher ſtill takes place. For, not to repeat the extraordinary caſe of the double births above ſtated, forty of the ſame breed of ewes, belonging to one of my neighbours, laſt year produced and fatted ſixty-ſeven lambs.

four pounds, which will pay rent with other expences, and ſtill leave a ſuperiority of profit over the cottager.

But it will be ſaid that none of my wethers are kept to be four years old, which our author conſiders of ſuch vaſt importance. To accommodate our reaſoning then to his peculiar ideas, I will put a caſe exactly in point. Suppoſe then a hundred ewes, for the purpoſe of breeding and bringing up lean wethers to four years old, previous to their being put to fatten, are kept upon twenty acres of land annually rented at a pound an acre, and that theſe hundred ewes produce a hundred wethers. With theſe the farmer will fold his arable grounds, more or leſs in quantity according to its ſoil and ſituation. In many parts of Hertfordſhire, and in ſome of Eſſex, beginning to fold at the end of March, and not leaving off till late in November, he will manure from 14 to 18 acres, worth from 20s. to 30s. each. In other places, on other ſoils, and in different ſeaſons, not beginning to fold till May, and finiſhing ſo early as the end of September or commencement of October, ſcarcely more than 10 or 12 of the ſame value would be covered. We will take the average number of acres at 12, and the average value per acre at 25s. This amounts to 15s. to every five ſheep; their wool at 4½ lb. a fleece, and 9d. per lb. makes upwards of 16s.; which, added to the 15s. manure, gives 1l. 11s. for the

the produce of the firſt year, excluſive of the value of the five wether lambs, *(f)* which are ſtill to be continued lean, and annually folded. The manure ariſing hence will not be greatly inferior, one year with another, to that of the firſt year; I will, however, only ſet it at 12s. annually. The wool will be conſiderably more, being nearly 6 lb. a fleece; which I may fairly eſtimate at a Todd the five, worth about a guinea. *(g)*

Some other of our author's ſtatements reſpecting the expences and profits of the farmer I might venture to conteſt; yet I will let them paſs, and our accounts will be nearly as under:

Farmer's

(f) An acre of the ſuppoſed land will keep five ſheep for folding, perhaps as well, as four when conſtantly fed upon it.

(g) The above reaſoning will be nearly the ſame, mutatis mutandis, whatever kind and ſize of ſheep are made uſe of. In Wilts and Hants, ſays a correſpondent from Somerſet, "Sheep "are uſually folded the whole year, and the fold of ewes and "lambs from a good meadow is extremely valuable, it "being the goodneſs of the feed upon which depend both "the quantity and worth of the dung. Eight hundred cou-"ples will cover an acre in a night, which may be fairly "eſtimated at 16s. often 20s. for the enſuing barley crop. "The ſummer dung decreaſes much in value, till two or three "weeks before wheat ſowing. Then again it increaſes, and, "where they can ſow immediately after the fold, the dung "of 1600 ſheep, which are ſufficient at that ſeaſon of the year "for an acre, is worth as much as the 800 couples were for "barley. To ſum up: I think the value of the manure ariſing "from

Farmer's Expences, &c.

	l.	s.	d.
Rent and pariſh rates four years - -	4	16	0
One fourth part of this for loſs by rot and accidents - - - - - -	1	4	0
Ditto for profit on labour and attention	1	4	0
Total expences	7	4	0
Total produce in wool and manure -	6	10	0
Remains - -	0	14	0

That is, the farmer can afford his four year old lean wethers at about three ſhillings per head.

COTTAGER.

As to our author's ſtatement of the cottager's expences, I abſolutely deny, ſome few extraordinary caſes excepted, his firſt and fundamental maxim, that he pays no rent for the privilege of commonage. *(b)* Our author's own poſitions and reaſonings, contrary to his intention, do themſelves inevitably prove it. He is very copious and eloquent in

" from 100 ſheep may be juſtly ſtated at about 15l. per annum. " In the county of Wilts, at leaſt, I know I am nearly right."

This account ſufficiently agrees with the above given eſtimates to afford them ſatisfactory confirmation.

(b) We ſhall hereafter ſee, that even granting that the cottager pays no rent for his right of commonage, and that it is in itſelf really a benefit, yet that it proves in the end, hurtful and pernicious.

diſplaying

difplaying the benefits arifing to a poor man from the neighbourhood of a large common. Grant them to be equal to his heightened rhetorical repre-fentation, to whom do thefe benefits belong? Do they belong to the proprietor of the cottage? If they do, and he lives in it himfelf, he immediately feels thefe benefits. If he lets or fells it, will he refign thefe benefits without an equivalent? You may as well fuppofe that the owner of a large eftate, endowed with common fenfe, will give it away for nothing.

But, fays this writer, the principal advantage of the right of common depends upon the dexterity of the commoner. Granted. Is it not the fame with regard to farms? But does the landlord efti-mate the value of them by the ignorance or folly of the farmer? Or by what may be fairly made of them by fkill and induftry? The latter is doubtlefs his ftandard of valuation. In like manner, if the renter of a cottage, in confequence of his vicinity to a common, can, by due care and management, keep five, ten, or twenty fheep upon it, the pro-prietor, fairly eftimating the profits of them, fixes the rent at 5, 10, or 20s. the more.

But our author has made it extremely uncertain, whether the cottager can actually enjoy thefe pri-vileges. " Though," fays he, " we have an unli-" mited right of commonage, and though we are

" not

" not bound by any manerial or parochial reſtric-
" tions to any particular quantity, or number of
" cattle reſpectively, our own *prudence governs* and
" *reſtrains us* on that head. We do not ſtock
" ourſelves with *more* cattle in the ſummer to feed
" on the commons, than we can properly keep at
" home in the winter." Now the ſame prudence which reſtrains the farmer from feeding *more* cattle on the commons in the ſummer, than he can properly keep at home in the winter, will it not as certainly induce him to keep as *many?* But if he does, what becomes of the poor man's ſheep? The farmer will keep as many as he conveniently can. If he takes in the cottager's, therefore he may chance to ſtarve both them and his own. Our Arcadian commoner, therefore, with his numerous flocks and herds, is, after all, reduced to a deſperate dilemma. If he ventures them on the common, this writer aſſures us, he frequently loſes many; if he ſends them to the farmer, the farmer has nothing to keep them with, he having already a ſufficient ſtock of his own. Either way the poor creatures muſt inevitably periſh. If they remain upon the dreary heath, they will ſtray away and be ſtolen; or die with cold, and wet, and hunger. If they go to the farmer, they muſt be ſtarved; with the only conſolation of a great many others being ſtarved along with them.

But

But there are ſtill other fallacies in the ſtatement of the cottager's accounts. The quantity of wool, if he keeps the ſame kind of ſheep, as is evidently ſuppoſed, will be a fourth part leſs than that of the farmer; and his loſſes by accidents will be a fourth part more.

Our author contends, indeed, that the cottager's ſheep are leſs liable to rot than the farmer's, as they will of themſelves, at the proper times, retire to the higher grounds. Now, unleſs the ſheep have more ſenſe than their maſter, the reverſe of this will generally happen. The farmer, of common diſcretion, will take care to keep his flocks, during a wet ſeaſon, in his drieſt fields and paſtures; whereas thoſe of the cottager, if at all inclined to rottenneſs, will often ſeek thoſe very ſpots, which tend to increaſe their diſorder: and will not this more eſpecially happen if (for the trifling profit of about a ſhilling a head) he lets them to fold upon the neighbouring fields of the farmer? Crouded together in the pen, will they not become conſiderably hot; and, upon being let out, will they not eagerly feed upon the moiſteſt herbage they can get, whether it be what immediately ſprings after haſty ſhowers, or ſuch as grows upon thoſe ſwamps and wet mooriſh lands, with which our waſtes and commons ſo much abound? Muſt not this naturally produce the fatal diſorder we are ſpeaking of? Nay, this ſudden tranſition from warm lodging to the bleak exposure of a heath, must likewise unavoidably subject them to colds, and that contagious distemper, called the scab; which as rapidly communicates itself to all the flocks upon the same common, as the small-pox or pestilence runs through a populous town; and although, by timely care, it prove not mortal, it often strips them of half their clothing, and leaves them poor, naked, and shivering, to the full operation of inclement seasons.

But after all, allowing the cottager's opportunity and convenience for keeping sheep, by the winter assistance of the farmer, let us here collect together the preceding observations and estimates, and place them before the reader in one view.

COTTAGER's EXPENCES.

	£.	s.	d.
Rent four years, at 5s. a year,	1	0	0
Keeping five ewes, producing five wether lambs, at a farmer's, 16 weeks in the winter, at 3d. a head,	1	0	0
Keeping the wethers 16 weeks, at 2d. a week per head, the three following winters,	2	0	0
Total gross cost,	4	0	0
Carried forward	4	0	0

	£	s.	d.
Brought forward	4	0	0
Add the fourth (*i*) of the groſs coſt for loſs' by rot, &c.	1	0	0
(*k*) Ditto for profits on labour and attention,	1	0	0
Total expences,	6	0	0

PROFITS.

	£	s.	d.
By wool, at even 2½ lb. per fleece, and 10d. a pound, about	2	2	0
Folding on the farmer's ground, at 1s. a head, during the beſt part of the ſummer,	1	0	0
Total profits,	3	2	0
Which deduct from the total expences, and there remains	2	18	0

Or about 11s. a head, at which the cottager can afford his four year old lean wether, which will not be nearly ſo good as what the farmer we have ſeen can afford for 3s.

In no way, then, does it appear, that the rearing of lean ſtock, by the aſſiſtance of *waſtes and com-*

(*i*) This might perhaps be fairly ſet at one third.

(*k*) This alſo, according to the preceding remarks, might be equally heightened.

mons,

mons, is but half as great as within rich enclosures. But granting for argument sake that it were, our author would still be very far from having proved, that the enclosures which have been made during the last thirty or forty years, have advanced the price of butcher's meat three halfpence in the pound more than the advance of price in other things. For, in order to establish this position, it would be necessary to ascertain the number of acres actually enclosed within the period now mentioned; what proportion they bear to *the wastes and commons* still uninclosed, as well to the whole quantity of land in Great-Britain, and how many cattle were kept before and since. None of these particulars has he shewn, or even attempted to shew. His estimate, therefore, of the necessary consequent advancement of butcher's meat, is mere random conjecture, unsupported by facts, or any just principles of reasoning.

Were I to form a judgment of the total number of acres contained in our recent enclosures, from the accounts of those I have now before me, I should not suppose they could exceed, if even amount to a million. But there can be little doubt, that more than four fifths of these were not *wastes* and *commons*, which chiefly affect the argument, but merely *open rented fields*. Supposing the lands of Great-Britain to be no more than sixty millions, the recent enclosure of *wastes* and *commons* cannot

be

be even a two hundredth part, a mere trifle, utterly insufficient to produce any sensible difference in the price of lean cattle, and consequently of butcher's meat.

Were it necessary I could very easily point out many other deficiencies and fallacies in our author's reasonings to establish the point now immediately before us. But from what has been already advanced, we may here very safely put an end to this part of our enquiry. We have seen that his statements to prove that the cottager can bring up lean stock upon commons and waste grounds at half the expence the farmer can upon his rich enclosures, are deficient in almost every possible particular; but that allowing them ever so full and complete, the deductions from them, *that our recent enclosures have raised the price of butcher's meat three halfpence in the pound more than the advance of price in other things*, is so far from true, they could not probably have raised it the fourth part of a farthing.

The high price of butcher's meat for the two or three years now immediately past, is, strictly speaking, no part of our enquiry. For, although our author in his title page mentions the *present* high price of it, yet he evidently means, both from the general tenour of his arguments, and from particular expressions occasionally used, several years preceding

ceding the publication of his pamphlet in the year 1785. The cause however of the high price of this article of provision even within the short period just now stated, being in itself a matter of considerable importance, it may not be amiss, before we proceed to our next general proposition, to say a few words respecting it.

Now I have not the smallest hesitation to assert. that it has arisen from a temporary *scarcity*, and that this scarcity has proceeded from a succession of *severe winters*, of *cold backward springs*, and *from a general failure of grass in the summers*. Was not the winter of 1783 so uncommonly sharp, that hay, in many parts of England, was 5l. a ton, and was not some exported to the continent at even nine (*k*)? Was it possible that the farmers could support their usual stock? Could the calves that fell early in the year 1784 be reared? Did not many of our cows, from being almost starved during the preceding months, miss their bulling, as the farmers express it? And was not again the winter of 1784 uncommonly long, as well as severe? Did not numbers of cattle die for want of fodder? And of those that lived, were not many so extremely poor as to make it impossible to fat them in the following summer, had grass been ever so plentiful? But unfortunately, was not

(*k*) Hay it seems then must have been dearer and scarcer with our neighbours than with us: Did this arise from *enclosures*?

the

the crop ſo exceſſively ſhort, that the farmers were diſtreſſed even to keep them at all? Was not the produce of barley too equally deficient? Did not that deficiency prevent the fatting vaſt numbers of hogs, which might otherwiſe in ſome meaſure have ſupplied the diminution of beef? And as to ſheep, what multitudes were ſtarved, ſome for want of hay, ſome for want of turnips, which were rotted and ſpoiled by the froſts? And of lambs, how many thouſands and tens of thouſands periſhed in the ſnows, or by the intenſeneſs of the cold? Are not we aſſured from the breeding counties, that their ſtocks, from theſe ſeveral cauſes, have been reduced $\frac{1}{6}$, $\frac{1}{5}$, and in ſome parts of Wales, unſheltered, unſecured, unfed, by encloſures, more than $\frac{1}{2}$? *(l)* In a word, are not both neat cattle and ſheep much fewer than in 1782? Muſt not theſe deficiencies be made up by the breeders before the graziers can expect lean ſtock to be plentiful and cheap, or the community hope for butcher's meat at prices moderate and eaſy?

Upon a view of all theſe concurrent cauſes, I am ſo far from being ſurpriſed at the temporary dear-

(l) This has the teſtimony of a capital farmer in South Wales, who alſo ſays, that, by the ſeverity of the late winters, their ſtocks both of cattle and ſheep, are become ſo exceedingly ſhort, that it will be ſome years before they will be able to ſell their uſual quantities. In that country there have been few or no *commons encloſed*; nay thouſands of ſheep periſhed for *want* of encloſures; (i. e.) for want of *ſhelter* and *winter food*.

neſs

neſs of theſe articles, that I am really aſtoniſhed they have riſen no higher, and cannot but conſider it as alone a ſtrong preſumption in favour of encloſures. Had not encloſures been more numerous and extenſive than they were fifty years ago, muſt not the price of beef and mutton have been greatly more advanced? Did not the ſingle hard winter of 1739, render them exceſſively dear, both through that ſeaſon, and the forty following ones? This appears in general from the beef table already given; and in perfect coincidence herewith is the information of a ſenſible farmer, of fifty years experience, a Mr. Thomas Fricker of Deverill Longbridge, Wilts, in anſwer to ſome queſtions ſent him on this ſubject. "In 1741, ſays he, beef ſold in the Dorſetſhire and "Wiltſhire markets at 6d. a pound:" and an acquaintance aſſures me upon his own particular recollection, "that about that time, at London, "the fineſt and choiceſt pieces for ſteaks fetched "even a ſhilling." I find alſo from a paragraph in a newſpaper, called the Conſtitutional Journal, that ſo late as April 30, 1743, at Frome in Somerſetſhire, pork was 5d. and all other meats 4½d. per pound. Theſe were the effects of *one* hard winter.

Have we not now had *two* or *three* in ſucceſſion? But in what county, at what country or city market has beef been a *ſhilling* or even *ſixpence* in the pound? "At ſeveral other periods," continues the above intelligent farmer, "beef has been both

"dear

" dear and ſcarce, and always from the ſame cauſe, "
" *ſevere winters and cold late ſprings*, which never
" fail to occaſion a ſcarcity of cattle."

Report of the LONDON COMMITTEE.

Before I quit this head, I cannot help taking notice of the *Report of the Committee appointed laſt ſummer, by the court of Common Council of London, to conſider the cauſes of the high prices of proviſions*. This *ſapient* body can ſurely never have been out of the ſmoke of the city. They ſeem to have known as little of the real condition of the country from which their proviſions are fetched, as philoſophers do of the world in the Moon. Nay ſuch appears to be the denſity of the atmoſphere that envelopes them, that no ray of truth, though coming with the force and brightneſs of the meridian ſun, can penetrate it. In ſpite of the aſſurances of reſpectable correſpondents from different parts of the kingdom that there was a real ſcarcity of fat ſheep and oxen; in ſpite of the manifeſt confirmation of this by the comparatively ſmall numbers brought to market, they aſcribe the dearneſs of meat to cauſes juſt as much concerned in it as Tenderden ſteeple was in the production of the Goodwin ſands. They impute it to jobbers, foreſtallers, regraters, &c. who neither *have* influenced, nor in a country of free competition like this, poſſibly *can* influence the price of theſe things, one hundredth part of a farthing in the pound, for three months together, in any market in the kingdom, especially those of London. But granting their operation ever so considerable, has it been *peculiarly* so during the two or three last years? Was it greater in 1784, 5, and 6 than in the years immediately preceding? One of the witnesses examined by the Committee, indeed, intimates that it was; but has that witness, or any other, produced the shadow of a proof, either from reason or fact? Another evidence, p. 22, asserts that although fewer beasts were brought to *Smithfield* in the years 1784 and 5 than the preceding ones, yet that the quantity driven up to *town* was nearly the same; but is not this flatly contradicted in the very same paragraph, where it is said that there were fewer there the last winter, for this manifest reason, that there was not a sufficient fodder to feed them? A Mr. Boys, a considerable salesman, roundly declares that about twenty years ago, "there used to "be a great many more beasts at Smithfield, so "that it would scarcely hold them all." But is not this declaration likewise shewn to be totally groundless by the table in p. 75, which contains the number of beasts and sheep annually brought thither for more than 50 years past? Does it not there appear that the average of the last six years was above a fifth part greater than that of the six years beginning with 1763?

But,

But, say the Committee, the excess of the London prices of meat over those of the country is more than double what would pay the expences and risque of sending, and that this must have arisen from forestalling, jobbing, &c. Ref. 3d, &c. From what evidence does this appear? By what calculation is it proved? As far as they have vouchsafed to communicate, does not the reverse stare us in the face? Are not these prices in some of the corporations where they applied for information even higher than those of London? Witness the accounts from York, Guilford, &c. Nay at this very day, and to come to my own county, I am assured that the price of beef at the markets of Rumford, Brentwood, Chelmsford, Walden, Epping is 5d. and 5½d. per lb. while I find by the public papers, that at those of Clare Hall, Leaden Hall, Newgate, &c. it is only 4½d. And has not the *advance* of price in all the places, where the requisite statements are given to the Committee, been also more *rapid?* Is not this strikingly apparent in the letters from Lincoln, Chichester, Portsmouth, Bury, Edinburgh, Stafford, Ely, &c.? But, allowing that the difference between the London and country prices equal to what is contended, must we, in order to account for it, necessarily have recourse to forestallers, jobbers, &c.? Was not this difference still greater in the years 1740, 41, and 42, than in 1784, 5, and 6? Was it *then* owing to these dreadful monsters, when all the laws against them were in full force? Has not *tallow*, and consequently *candles*, been considerably more raised than even beef and mutton? Has this too been occasioned by the jobbers and forestallers of Smithfield?

But enclosures likewise seem to come in for a share in the Committee's heavy accusations. But how is this charge supported? Why, they procure a list of the enclosures made in the twelve years, ending with 1786, containing almost 500,000 acres; and it appears that upon 250,000 of these acres, sheep were forbidden to be depastured for ten or twelve years. Their conclusion from hence, I suppose, is, that our number of sheep must have been diminished, and the price of butcher's meat of course considerably heightened. But how fallacious! For what were these enclosures? What change took place in the cultivation or management of the lands? Was it of arable to pasture, or of pasture to arable? What were the products before and since? None of these things are we told; and yet *without* these, all the rest how little to the purpose? Of those from which sheep were excluded were not a great part mere arable common fields? And how many sheep, let me ask, were maintained upon fallows and alternate stubbles of wheat and barley and oats? And as to those from which sheep were *not* excluded, is it not notorious that many of them converted tillage into pasture,

paſture, and that they now ſupport twenty ſheep and oxen inſtead of one? And of thoſe which were paſture before and are paſture ſtill, do not ſome, as in inſtances already given, produce three times as much butcher's meat as they ever uſed to do? Nay, is it not ſtrikingly evident from the tables the Committee themſelves have given us in Numbers III. and V. of the Appendix to their Report, that their apprehenſions are totally groundleſs? For does it not there appear, that thoſe very years in which the moſt numerous and extenſive encloſures took place, and the three or four immediately ſubſequent ones, the greateſt numbers of both ſheep and oxen were driven to Smithfield?

The Committee having, as they fancied, found out the cauſes of the complained of evils, proceed, with no leſs ſagacity, to preſcribe the remedies; remedies, which if they could command mild winters, and fruitful ſummers, or make ſheep and oxen come down from the ſkies, we might have halcyon days; but if not, the only tendency, of three-fourths of them, is to do eſſential miſchief; they are fitted to increaſe the calamities they were intended to remove, and, if poſſible, would finally drive the market from Smithfield, as I am told, regulations of ſimilar diſcernment have driven that from Saliſbury, which uſed to be one of the beſt country markets in the kingdom.

A few years ago the learned Academicians of Paris and Soissons * assembled to consider of the best method of encouraging and promoting the growth of turnips in France. One of these gentlemen having been in England, had thoroughly informed himself with respect to the excellent mode of cultivating this vegetable practised in Norfolk. This mode he states to the assembly with great perspicuity and precision. But another of the members, a man of high conceit and fluent elocution, pours such irresistible contempt upon this information of English origin, that no further attention is paid to it. This powerful persuasive orator and his brethren, with a solemn formality suited to the importance of the occasion, proceed to draw up a set of rules and prescriptions, for directing the culture in question. Some of these regulations are admirably calculated to prevent the turnips growing at all, and the rest, should the turnips happen to flourish in spite of every effort to destroy them, are no less excellent for rendering the growth itself of little or no value.

Perfectly similar to this appears to have been the conduct of our London Committee. They gravely pretend to enquire into the causes of the high price of provisions, and in order the better to succeed in this enquiry, they examine witnesses, and dispatch letters into different parts of the kingdom, request-

* Annals of Agriculture.

ing information and aſſiſtance. But what uſe do they make of the intelligence procured? Why, that which accords with their own preconceptions they readily adopt and lay wonderful ſtreſs upon; that of a contrary kind, however rational in itſelf, and however well ſupported by facts, they ſeem to paſs over as utterly inſignificant. As this is evidently the caſe with reſpect to the evidence of ſome of the witneſſes, and with reſpect likewiſe to ſome of the letters from mayors of corporations already referred to, ſo is it eſpecially with regard to one written to a member of the Committee by Mr. Arthur Young, which, for the acuteneſs of penetration, and extenſive knowledge of the real ſtate of things in the country, it ſo clearly manifeſts, is worth all the letters of all the mayors of corporations put together. This is neither noticed in any of their reaſonings and obſervations, nor even vouchſafed a place in their report. The obvious concluſions hence deducible, I leave to the public.

When I read the rules and preſcriptions of the French Academicians, I feel, I confeſs, a ſtrong propenſity to ridicule; but when I peruſe the report of the London Committee, and conſider myſelf as a member of the ſame general ſociety, I can ſcarcely reſtrain the emotions of ſerious indignation. I am, indeed, ſhocked to behold men of liberal education, and truly reſpectable characters,

become

become the dupes of prejudices, which, I fondly imagined, had disgraced only the lowest of the vulgar.

I have never known wheat uncommonly dear, but I have as constantly heard violent clamours from the ignorant poor against their superiors for sending corn abroad to feed their enemies; whereas the fact in these cases has always been, that, instead of *sending* it abroad, we have, as fast as we could, been *fetching* it thence, that the ungrateful murmurers might not be starved. Candour and humanity, however, will readily palliate, if not entirely excuse, such apparent ingratitude. They are destitute of the means for obtaining the requisite intelligence properly to judge in the case, and, therefore, very naturally follow the impulse of passion excited by misapprehension. But where is the candour, where is the ingenuity that can frame an adequate apology for parallel conduct in the London Committee? Have they not, in direct opposition to the clearest evidence, charged the inflictions of heaven upon the knavery and villainy of innocent individuals. Have they not been devising fines, and penalties, and punishments against their greatest benefactors? Against men who have ransacked the country in every quarter to find them provisions? Have bought them sheep and cattle, even at extravagant rates, to keep them from starving? To feed our capital, that ever *growing*, yet ever

ever *grumbling* monſter, which, like the daughters of the horſeleach, mentioned in the Proverbs, is perpetually crying, "give, give," and never ſaying, it is enough. Nay, have not ſolemn reſolutions been formed to apply to parliament for the revival of laws which were long the diſgrace of our ſtatute book, but which, upon an application, adviſed by one of the greateſt and wiſeſt men *(m)* this kingdom ever produced, were, but a few years ago, happily repealed? Had the ſummer of 1786 been as dry as that of 1784 and 5, and the winter now paſt as ſevere as that of 1783, dreadful muſt have been the deficiency of ſheep and oxen, and exceſſively high the prices of meat; and, under the impreſſion of thoſe ideas which our committee ſeems zealous to propagate, what riots, and tumults, and confuſion might have enſued?

(m) Lord Mansfield.

SECTION III.

Granting that our recent Enclosures have advanced the Price of Butcher's Meat three Halfpence in the Pound more than the advance of Price in other Things; yet the Enclosure of all our Wastes and Commons could not raise it to Nine-pence or a Shilling.

THIS proposition requires no laboured reasoning to establish. Our author has himself, indeed, sufficiently proved it. The farmer, says he, can afford to sell his lean cattle, reared upon rich enclosures of 20s. an acre, at the rate of sixpence a pound. Were therefore *all the wastes* and *commons* enclosed and rendered equally rich and fertile, on his own principles, sixpence a pound would still be the price the farmer could afford it at, and at which, consequently, it would be bought. What then becomes of the nine-pence or a shilling? Both are vanished.

But supposing it otherwise; supposing, that although upon our present enclosures of 20s. an acre, lean cattle may be raised for six-pence a pound; yet, were all the lands enclosed, and rendered of the same value, it would inevitably happen,

pen, by ſome magic or other, beyond all human comprehenſion, that it could not be done for leſs than nine-pence or a ſhilling, what would be the conſequence? This writer has himſelf very kindly ſuggeſted it. *Lean cattle would be imported from abroad.* Every country in Europe, which breeds them, long before they aroſe to ſo enormous a price, would be emulous to furniſh us with them at a much lower rate; and our produce of corn would be proportionably increaſed. Both ways, therefore, our author helps to defeat his own arguments, and to ſhew that his aſſertions, reſpecting the univerſal encloſure of our waſte lands, cannot be true.

Before I proceed to our next propoſition, I muſt beg leave to preſent an argument, ſimilar to that we have been conſidering, and which I cannot but wonder has eſcaped our author's penetration, to prove that encloſures have already encreaſed the price of *horſes*, ſeven or eight hundred per cent. and that, ſhould all our waſte grounds be encloſed, this price would be double what it is at preſent. It is very well known, that, upon ſome of our foreſt lands, horſes are now bred wild, the peculiar property of nobody. When three or four years old, they are, from time to time, caught by the lazier part of the poor people in the neighbourhood, (who are fonder of the frolic of *horſe hunting* than of regular induſtrious labour) and ſold for what they can get. You may ſometimes purchaſe a tolerable nag of them for three or four ſhillings and a mug of beer; and, at all events, you may be almoſt ſure of one for 20s. which will do you eminent ſervice, and ſuch as could not be brought up by the farmer on his rich encloſures of 20s. an acre for leſs than eight or ten guineas. Conſequently our recent encloſures have encreaſed the price of horſes in the proportion of at leaſt eight or ten to one; and ſhould all our waſtes and commons be encloſed, as is reported to be the intention of government, the preſent high price would be doubled. Before our author indulges his ridicule at the egregious abſurdity of this reaſoning, let me intreat him to remember that it is exactly his own, thoſe particulars only excepted, in which it is ſuperiour.

SECTION IV.

Granting that the universal Enclosure of our Wastes and Commons would advance the Price of Butcher's Meat to Nine-pence or a Shilling in the Pound, it would by no means be a conclusive Objection against such Enclosure. (a)

ALLOWING that the universal enclosure of our wastes, &c. would produce the asserted effect, yet still, before the argument against such enclosure were compleat, it must be shewn that this disadvantage more than counterbalanced the various certain benefits, which, in other respects would arise from it. Our author has indeed attempted this; but, in my apprehension, very unsuccessfully.

(a) " Granting the assertion, that where cattle are bred upon " heaths and commons," observes a correspondent, " the tenants are enabled to sell them cheap, because they have such " lands for little or no rent; can it be reasonable that those " few counties in which they still remain, should have the exclusive privilege of breeding cattle cheaper than the inclosed " parts of the kingdom, unless it could be proved they could " breed sufficient for the whole nation? Or is it equitable " that the owners of estates, entitled to such rights of common, should be obliged to forego the improvement of such " estates, when they have it in their power to double or " treble the value of them by an enclosure?"

ſucceſsfully. That I may fairly meet and encounter his calculations made for this purpoſe, I will here ſtate them in their full force and magnitude.

He ſays, p. 93, that, " ſuppoſing there are " ten millions of inhabitants in Great-Britain;" (which is indeed pretty near the fact) " and that " each inhabitant, one with another, conſumes " one quarter of a pound of meat per day, the " advanced price of three halfpence in the pound, " which has already taken place in conſequence of " encloſures, is equivalent to a tax upon the na- " tion at large, of *five millions ſterling per annum*." Reſuming the ſubject in page 102, he obſerves, " that admitting butcher's meat, in conſequence " of the univerſal encloſure of waſtes, &c. would " be four-pence halfpenny dearer than at preſent, " it would be an additional burden of *fifteen mil-* " *lions ſterling per annum*. But as the lower claſſes " of people would be in a great meaſure deprived " of eating butcher's meat, there would not pro- " bably be more than one-third part conſumed " there is at preſent; therefore the eſtimate of " *fifteen millions per annum*, ſhould be reduced to " *five millions per annum*." Now admitting the general reſult of this computation, I am not at all afraid but that I ſhall be able to prove, that the advantages ariſing from the propoſed encloſure, would more than counterbalance this burden,

burden, heavy as it would be, and partly too, from this writer's own conceſſions.

He acknowledges, p. 22, " that ſhould the ge-" neral cultivation of the waſte lands be adopted, " we ſhould moſt probably produce a great deal " more corn than would be required for home con-" ſumption;" but notwithſtanding this, in oppoſition to common ſenſe, and in ſpite of every day's experience, he is confident " that the price of " grain would be nearly the ſame, neither much " dearer nor much cheaper than at preſent." And the reaſon given for this extraordinary opinion is, " that we ſhould ſend the overplus abroad, and " conſequently the price at *home*, would be the " ſame which the merchant could ſell it for " *abroad*, deducting the charge of tranſporta-" tion." The ſimple fact, as apparent in the following table, is alone a ſufficient refutation of this curious reaſoning.

Quantities of Wheat and Barley exported from and imported into England and Scotland for 14 years from the 5th of January 1771, to the 5th of January 1784, with their average Prices each Year respectively, the former extracted from the Custom House Books, the latter from the Corn Register established by Act the 10th of Geo. III.

Years.	WHEAT AND FLOUR.			BARLEY AND MALT.		
	Exported Quarters.	Imported Quarters.	Prices of Wheat per Qur.	Exported Quarters.	Imported Quarters.	Prices of Barley per Qur.
1771	10,089	2,510	47s. 2d	34,198	228	25s. 8d
1772	6,959	25,474	50 8	14,031	3,068	25 4
1773	7,637	56,857	51 0	2,471	63,916	28 4
1774	15,928	289,149	52 8	2,911	171,508	28 6
1775	91,037	560,988	48 4	51,414	139,451	26 0
1776	210,664	20,578	38 2	136,114	8,499	20 2
1777	87,686	233,323	45 6	142,725	7,981	20 6
1778	141,070	106,394	42 0	103,930	42,714	22 8
1779	222,261	5,039	33 8	85,777	7,085	19 6
1780	224,059	3,915	35 8	191,563	352	17 0
1781	103,021	159,866	44 8	150,468	56	17 2
1782	145,152	80,695	47 10	127,744	13,592	22 6
1783	51,943	584,183	52 8	54,065	144,926	30 4
1784	89,288	216,947	48 10	66,889	77,182	27 10
14 Yrs.	1,406,794	2,345,918 1,406,794	45 8 Average Price.	1,164,304 680,558	680,558	23 8 Average Price per Quarter.
Balance	Imported	939,124				
Balance	Exported			483,746		

Upon the most superficial view of this Table it cannot but forcibly strike the observer that every year in which the exports greatly exceeded the imports the price of both wheat and barley was extremely

extremely moderate; whereas when the imports confiderably exceeded the exports, the price was exceffively high. Thus for inftance, in the years 1779 and 1780, when the exports had greatly the lead, the joint average price of wheat was fcarcely 35s. a quarter, but in the years 1773, 1774 and 1783, when the imports fo much prevailed, the medium price was upwards of 52s. a quarter; confequently the price of wheat in years of great exportation is 17s. a quarter cheaper than in thofe of great importation. We alfo find, upon the beft information that can be procured, that for nineteen years together, that is from 1746 to 1765, when the exports of corn fo far exceeded the imports that the nett gain was 651,000l. a year, the average price of wheat was little more than 32s. a quarter. Should exportations again equally prevail, from whatever caufe, it feems inevitably to follow, nor does there appear the fhadow of a reafon for fuppofing the contrary, after every allowance made, that the average price of wheat would not much exceed 35s. a quarter. Lower than that it ought not to be fuffered to fink. Otherwife the farmer could not afford to grow it; and fo the very caufe which reduced the price, would prevent the production, and finally operate to effects directly contrary.

Now the average price of wheat during the fourteen years given in the preceding table is 45s. a quarter, and it further appears from the Cuftom

House books, that the grain imported in the same period has cost the nation 330,000l. per annum. *(b)* Partly on this writer's own concessions, therefore, the following advantages would result from the proposed enclosure of our wastes and commons; First, There would be an annual saving of 330,000l. from the prevention of importation. 2dly, There would be a considerable sum arising from the sale of corn sent abroad: my only doubt in this case is, that scarcely any extent of cultivation could always secure this. And 3dly, Our wheat would be 10s. a quarter cheaper for our total home consumption. All these put together would, it is presumed, go a great way towards a compensation for the 4½d per lb. which our author asserts (though very unjustly we have seen) would be added to the price of butcher's meat.

The last article alone, the diminution of the price of wheat, at the rate of 10s. a quarter for all our people, would be a prodigious benefit. For allowing with our author that there are ten millions of inhabitants in Great Britain, and supposing, (what I presume cannot be above the fact,) that

(b) The decrease of exportation has arisen from an increase of that best of all markets, a home consumption, occasioned by the vast increase of our people, and of our horses; both which are perhaps equal to an additional annual growth of two millions of quarters of wheat, and three or four millions of quarters of oats, beans and barley.

each

each inhabitant, one with another, consumed eight bushels of wheat in a year, this would be 10s. a year saved to each individual, and five millions sterling to the whole kingdom; which, the advantage of it resulting more immediately to the poor, would directly and powerfully operate as an encouragement to our agriculture and manufactures of every sort; whereas the price of butcher's meat, affecting chiefly the middle and higher ranks, would in this respect, have comparatively very considerable influence.

But these are a small part of the advantages which would probably arise from the measure we are speaking of. For I must here venture in the first place, to adopt part of Mr. Lamport's computations, notwithstanding the pleasantry and ridicule which our author has so plentifully poured upon them. *(c)* " The lands of Great Britain," says Mr. L. " are computed at seventy-two millions of " acres; Mr. Eden estimates the *rental* of them at " twenty millions; according to Mr. Young, the " average rent of an acre, is eleven shillings and " four pence to the land owner. From these data " it appears, that we have between 35 and 36 mil" lions of acres under cultivation, either meadow " pasture or arable, to which add, (which is a good " deal too much) twenty millions for houses, gar" dens, woods, parks, lawns, rivers, swamps, roads

(c) Pol. Enq. &c. p. 36.

" and barren ſpots, and there will remain at leaſt " ſixteen millions of acres, nearly one quarter of " the kingdom, capable of improvement, though " at preſent in the ſame ſtate they were found in " by Julius Cæſar."

" The cultivated lands," continues Mr. Lamport, " are ſuppoſed to produce three *rentals*." I muſt beg leave here to obſerve if the lands are about $\frac{1}{3}$ paſture and $\frac{2}{3}$ds arable, which is perhaps nearly the average proportion for the whole kingdom, and they are let at only moderate rents, not leſs than *four rentals* will enable the farmer to get a decent livelihood, and make a proper proviſion for his family. *Three* might be ſufficient forty years ago, but I am perſuaded, from repeated obſervation, and numerous enquiries, that ſuch are the neceſſarily encreaſed expences attending the farming buſineſs, from a variety of cauſes, by no means requiſite here to be ſtated, that *four* are but barely adequate. In ſome kinds of culture, it muſt be vaſtly greater; in that of hops for inſtance, if the produce be not equal to eight or ten rentals, the growth of them cannot be continued. I may therefore ſafely venture to ſet the neceſſary average produce at *four* rentals. *(d)*

" If

(d) In Mr. Young's Annals of Agriculture, No. 29, p. 425, I find Mr. Macro's annual expences, including the intereſt of ſtock, upon a farm of 415l. a year, and containing 1000 acres of land, 100 paſture and 900 arable, were 2208l. 2s. 6d. or nearly

" If the whole lands may be made," continues Mr. Lamport's argument, " to produce one-fifth " (e) part more, the rental of the land owners will " then amount to twenty-four millions, and the " produce to the nation at four rentals to the ad- " ditional ſum of ſixteen millions; what may " not this effect in the article of taxes, &c. eſpe- " cially when all its operation has been exerted in " trading with it!"

Now, allowing the accuracy of Mr. L—'s eſtimates reſpecting the number of acres in Great-Britain, the average rent per acre of ſuch part as is cultivated, the number of acres now under cultivation, and the proportion of waſte ground capa-

nearly $5\frac{1}{2}$ rents. In No. 32. p. 159 of the ſame uſeful work, Mr. William Hall, of Elmſtone in Kent, ſtates the annual expence of his farm, rented at 350l. and containing 306 acres, about half arable and half paſture, at 1231l. 10s. or about $3\frac{1}{2}$ rents. Theſe accounts ſufficiently confirm the above eſtimate.

(e) This is ſo far from being an extravagant ſuppoſition with reſpect to the kingdom at large, that I may ſafely venture to aſſert with regard to the beſt and oldeſt cultivated counties in England, ſuch as Norfolk, Suffolk, Eſſex, &c. that they produce one-fifth part more corn than they did forty years ago; nor is there any abſurdity in hoping that in 40 to come, by due attention and improvements, the encreaſe may be one-fifth part more. But if this may be the caſe with the higheſt cultivated counties, what may be expected from thoſe that abound with waſtes and commons?

ble of improvement, I ſee no material objection to his concluſions, except it be that he has forgot to compute the produce of the waſte lands, and that he appears alſo to have included the rents he all along ſuppoſes to be given for rights of common in the twenty millions rental of the cultivated grounds. Both theſe ought certainly to have been deducted; but then it is to be remembered, that he has ſet the proportion of the produce to the rent ſo much too low as to be more than a compenſation for this, and we may therefore allow with Mr. L—, that the total increaſed produce of the ſixteen millions of improvable acres yet to be incloſed, provided they prove only half as fertile, *(f)* (which is the utmoſt his argument ſeems to require, notwithſtanding what our author ſays *(g)* to the contrary) as thoſe already under cultivation, would be at leaſt twelve millions ſterling per annum.

But our author having ſtrangely imagined that Mr. L. had aſſerted, that our preſent waſte lands, when encloſed and cultivated, would be of equal fertility with thoſe already under culture, moſt wonderfully diverts himſelf with his own fancy, as the mere reverie and pleaſant dream of Mr.

(f) Curſ. Rem. p. 52.

(g) Polit. Enq. p. 52.

L. *(h)* And yet, ſuppoſing this aſſertion really to have been made, he has not advanced even the ſhadow of an argument to ſhew its abſurdity.

He ſays, indeed, what Mr. L. and all the world readily allow, that ſome lands may be incapable of culture ſo as to anſwer the expence, but he ſhould have recollected that theſe are comprehended in the twenty millions of acres, ſuppoſed for ever to remain uninclosed and uncultivated. As to the reſt, he ſeems chiefly to rely upon the imagined *wiſdom of our anceſtors*, *(i)* which directed them, he ſuppoſes, to the moſt judicious choice of what land ſhould be cultivated, and what ſhould be left waſte; and, in proof of this *antient wiſdom*, he maintains that the preſent waſtes, excepting ſome few inſtances, bear no compariſon in point of *natural* quality with thoſe which are already in a ſtate of cultivation. As to the choice made by our anceſtors, I fancy it was oftener directed by chance than ſkill; and the whole of this argument, if it may be called one, might be carried back to any indefinite period; a hundred, five hundred, a thouſand or even two thouſand years, till we got amongſt our naked ſavage forefathers; and had it always been adopted, we ſhould ſtill have remained as rude, as naked, as

(h) Polit. Enq. p. 34.

(i) Polit. Enq. p. 52.

ſavage as they. But not to retire into the remote ages of antiquity, what would have been the conſequence had it prevailed only *thirty years* ago? Are not thoſe barren waſtes which have ſince been cultivated now as fertile upon an average as our oldeſt encloſures? Nay, are not many of them, (eſpecially in the counties of Leiceſter, Lancaſter, Worceſter, Glouceſter, Somerſet, Lincoln, &c. ten times as productive as before? And can our author prove, has he even attempted to prove, that there are not really ſixteen millions of acres ſtill uninclosed, altogether as promiſing? Was there even a ſingle ſpot of them equal in *natural* richneſs of ſoil to a great part of New Foreſt in Hampſhire, which the *wiſdom of our anceſtors* depopulated, *(k)* "though covered "with numberleſs villages for thirty miles in ex- "tent, contained thirty *(l)* mother churches be- "ſide many ſubordinate ones, and nearly an hun- "dred thouſand acres of the beſt cultivated land "in the kingdom." When we hear that commiſſioners are appointed to enquire into the ſtate of this diſtinguiſhed territory, as well as others of ſimilar kind, what heart does not glow at the delightful proſpect which ſeems to ariſe! Who does not ſee the *wilderneſs become a fruitful field*; the

(k) See Lord Egmont's pamphlet on the encloſure of the foreſt lands.

(l) By the map of the county it appears now to contain only ſeven of every kind.

heaven-

heaven-directed spires again to *rise*, and the whole wide extent to people fast, not with beasts of chace, as heretofore, to please a savage tyrant, but with industrious men and women, rational creatures, happy subjects of the best of kings, and candidates for immortality! *(m)*

But to keep the present argument full before us, only grant that there yet remains sixteen millions of acres of uncultivated land; (which our author seems to have no objection to,) and allow it may be rendered as productive as that under present culture, (against which idea nothing has been advanced of the smallest importance,) and I see no absurdity in supposing that the consequence of the general enclosure would be not merely what Mr. Lamport contends, an additional *twelve millions*, but an additional *twenty-four millions*.

Nay, I stop not even here. The most valuable productions of improved agriculture are not wheat and barley, sheep and oxen; but human creatures; which, if I may be allowed the expression, as na-

(m) In the southern and eastern part of the forest, there are now, it seems, some fertile, well cultivated spots. But through almost the whole of the northern, our author might see his *happy* commoners very little superior to Hottentots, and crawling out of their huts, with scarcely any thing to cover their nakedness, or to defend them from the inclemency of the weather but a piece of old sacking tied about their middle.

turally ſpring from a melioration of the earth as corn and graſs, as trees, as plants, and flowers. The population of the thirty-ſix millions of acres already in culture is allowed to be ten millions. The remaining ſixteen millions rendered equally rich and prolific, muſt produce a population of at leaſt four millions more, which conſidered in the food they would eat, the clothes they would wear, the tools they would uſe, and the fuel they would burn, could not be of leſs annual value to the ſtate than 10l. a head; that is, in the whole, an addition of forty millions ſterling per annum.

All this is perhaps infinitely ſhort of what would be the fact, were ideas directly oppoſite to our author's univerſally to animate the minds of our people, and improvements correſpondent to, and indeed connected with, encloſures, generally to take place. We ſhall probably have a glimpſe of this when we ſtate and examine our author's miſcellaneous objections to the general encloſure, &c. But already I conſider the purpoſe of this ſection, as well as that of the three preceding ones, ſufficiently accompliſhed. We have ſeen, 1ſt, That butcher's meat is not encreaſed three halfpence in the pound during the laſt thirty years, more than other things. 2dly, That granting this, it cannot have ariſen from the encloſures which have been made in that time. 3dly, Allowing both the one and the other, that the general encloſure of waſte lands would not

raiſe

raise the price of butcher's meat four-pence half-penny more. And, 4thly, Admitting even all the three propositions, that the argument thence deduced against such enclosure would not be conclusive.

These several points being, in my apprehension, fully established, I shall next consider a few miscellaneous objections, and with them conclude.

SECTION V.

Miscellaneous Objections considered.

---

1. *Right of Common, a Privilege and Happiness to the Poor.*

THE trite and common objections to enclosures, that they are inevitably a violation of private property, and a great diminution of the privileges and happiness of the poor, have been sufficiently answered in an elegant well written pamphlet, *printed for and sold by P. Sandford, Shrewsbury, in the year* 1781.

With respect, however, to the latter of these objections, as our author has thought proper, with earnest zeal, to revive it, I must not entirely pass it over in silence. After describing the primeval bliss of his Arcadian commoners, the peace and innocence, the virtue and industry with which they conduct their lives, he adds, p. 115, "I cannot "but own, that I myself have some degree of "pleasure in finding a cottager possessed of the "means of making a gift to a new-born child, "of a live ewe lamb as a portion; because I have "known instances, when *a lucky* child has found "itself, at the end of ten or twelve years of age, "hereby in possession of perhaps half a score, or "a dozen ewes and wethers, the produce of whose "wool, &c. has found the child *in pocket-money* "till she has arrived at 18 or 20 years of age; "this *little* flock, together with her own *little* "*earnings*, has served as a portion with her to an "industrious young man who marries her, and "which has greatly contributed to support their "children." This is all to be sure very fine! Let me ask, however, had this lovely *shepherdess* gone to a good service at the age of fifteen, and continued in it eight or ten years, and then married, might she not have brought her *industrious young man* 20 or 30l.? And would not this have been a better portion than all her *childish pocket-money, her little flock and her little earnings?*

In

In opposition to our author's eloquent description, I beg leave to state the following plain and simple fact. A farmer's servant in this neighbourhood, when at the age of about twenty-five, which is now sixteen years ago, married a decent, worthy young woman scarcely turned of twenty. He neither received the marriage dower now mentioned, nor had he flocks and herds, sheep or lambs, cows or calves, or any PARADISAICAL common; yet, by the labours of husbandry alone, he has supported a family of four children, two boys and two girls. The elder of the sons, being past fifteen, is out at service, the younger, nearly fourteen, works with his father, while the two daughters assist their mother. By permission of the lord of the manor, in the year 1781, he fenced in a small piece of ground by the highway side, and built him a house upon it, which consists of two neat apartments on the lower floor, and as many above, and has at the end, a commodious brew-house. To render every domestic occupation perfectly convenient, it has since been surrounded by various little out-buildings, insomuch that there is now not only a hog's cote, and a house for wood, but a hut to receive the spinning wheels and other utensils, even a shed to shelter the necessary provisions for a sow and pigs, and also a well secured bee-stall, filled with hives. The yard containing about ten or twelve square rods, is excellently ſenced by a quick-hedge, which is already ſtrong and vigorous. On one ſide of the yard are planted apple-trees of different ſorts, on another plumb-trees, and cherry-trees of as various kinds. The intermediate ſpace, before the *encloſure*, was part of it a mere gravel pit, and the reſt ſo utterly barren as never to have half filled the belly of a ſingle ſheep or even rabbit. But now, from proper culture and ſuitable manure, it yields beans, peas, fine potatoes, and other uſeful garden productions in vaſt abundance; *(a)* a thrifty grape vine too, promiſing many a comfortable reviving cordial for declining years, has already ſpread its mantling branches a conſiderable way round the walls of the houſe. This rural manſion, with its ſeveral appurtenances, all in firm and perfect repair, can be worth very little leſs than 40l.; and I am informed on good authority, that the honeſt diligent man has already laid by nearly enough to raiſe another of ſimilar value, ſhould a like opportunity preſent. I muſt confeſs I never paſs this *houſe of Induſtry* without feeling the higheſt pleaſure. I yeſterday evening, the 11th of Auguſt 1786, made it a viſit. The father and the ſecond ſon were returning from the labours of harveſt. In the language of the poet, *The buſy houſe-wife was plying her even-*

(a) A picture in miniature of ſuch encloſures as have converted graſs to arable, and which have been properly managed.

ing's

ing's care; and though the daughters were too big *to run and lisp her sire's return, and climb his knees the envied kiss to share*; yet, what was ample amends, heart-felt joy appeared in every face, and their wholesome supper was eaten with a relish, I ween, which the rich and the great but seldom know. No more let us hear of *happy commoners* and the wondrous *rights* of *commonage*.

Instances similar to the above are given us by the ingenious Mr. Arthur Young, in his very useful Annals of Agriculture, No. 26, p. 177. "The "little village in which I live, says he, has two "labourers who have saved enough to become "farmers, and a third who has spent 60l. in build-"ing himself a tiled and bricked cottage." A man might, I presume gallop over all the heaths and commons in England before he would meet with many examples of this kind from the *privileges* of *commonage*.

In good earnest, if these privileges are really and finally so advantageous to the poor, as is pretended, the poor must certainly be in the most comfortable condition where these privileges are most extensive, and a satisfactory proof of it must as certainly appear in the lightness of the poor rates. Now, as far as my own observation has reached, or as I have been able to collect authentic intelligence from others,

others, the fact is generally the reverse. Seldom have I passed over an extensive waste, but I have been shocked with the sight of a proportionable number of half-naked, half-starved women and children, with pale meagre faces, peeping out of their miserable huts, or lazing and lounging about after a few paltry screaming geese, or scabby worthless sheep; and as seldom have I found, upon enquiry, that the parochial assessments were not excessively high. "At Chailey, in Sussex, where "there are miles of commons, upon which the "poor have flocks and herds, the parish rates, "instead of being extremely light, are chiefly from "this very cause, 9s. in the pound." *(b)*

In the parish of Sutton Coldfield in Warwickshire, an ingenious and very obliging correspondent assures me, there are several thousand acres of common, upon which every poor family in the place has the right of commonage, and some individuals keep even twenty sheep a-piece. Besides this, five or six hundred acres are successively enclosed every four or five years, and an acre allotted to each, which he lets or cultivates as he thinks most convenient or profitable. At the expiration of this term, the fences are thrown down, and the land again becomes common, with the feed very much improved from the temporary cul-

(b) Annals of Agriculture, No. 27, p. 221.

tivation it has had, and a ſimilar encloſure of another part of the common immediately ſucceeds. So that the poor have here a double advantage; the privilege of turning their little ſtock upon the common at large, and the allotment of an acre in the temporary encloſure, of which they frequently make a guinea annual rent. And what is remarkable, and particularly to our preſent argument, theſe advantages have greatly increaſed within the laſt thirty or forty years; the allotments having been enlarged from half an acre to a whole one, and the improvement in the cultivation having rendered the ſame quantity of double value. Here then ſurely we ſhall find the poor in a moſt comfortable condition, and ſcarcely any burthen at all to the pariſh. Juſt the contrary. The total annual expence of maintaining them was,

In 1742-3 only	£. 195	1	3
In 1766-7	514	18	0
In 1781-2	816	0	0
In 1785-6 even	1025	3	0

Parochial aſſeſſments, indeed, within the compaſs of time here ſtated have been doubled throughout the kingdom, and in ſome particular places, even more; but I do not recollect a ſingle inſtance, large manufacturing towns excepted, where, as here, they have been multiplied more than *five* times. Part of this prodigious increaſe is, perhaps, to be aſcribed to the increaſe of population, which is now almoſt twice as great as in the year 1740; I am ſtrongly apprehenſive, however, that it has chiefly ariſen from the very great and unuſual privileges above deſcribed. Servants, &c. in the heighbourhood, allured by theſe temptations, try every ſtratagem in order to gain a ſettlement in ſo flattering a ſituation. Hence an influx of inhabitants more than adequate to the increaſed employment; the want of which the rights of common cannot compenſate.

Had all the waſte lands in this pariſh, capable of improvement, been gradually incloſed between the years 1740 and 1750, and remained ſo to this day; had the proper allotments been made to each perſon, and every one who was able cultivated his own, or accepted a due compenſation, with the perpetual extinction of all future claims, the population, I am confident, from the vaſtly augmented employment, would have been greater than even it is now, and I am inclined to think that the poor rates would not have been ſo high by one third. On the contrary, if things are managed as they have hitherto been, or even twice the quantity of temporary incloſure ſhould be allowed, I ſhould not wonder if the parochial expences, in the courſe of twenty years, are more than double their preſent amount.

For even fixt and perpetual benefits to the poor of a pariſh, though in themſelves clear and certain, yet, viewed in their connections and conſequences are often highly injurious. In the pariſh of Debenham in Suffolk there is a charity eſtate of 200l. a year for the uſe of the poor, and the pariſh of Framlingham, in the ſame county, has one of even 1000l. and yet in each the poor rates are 4s. 6d. in the pound; whereas in the neighbouring pariſh of Aſpal, which has no ſuch deluſive advantage, they are ſcarcely 1s. 6d. "Give the poor," ſays the ſprightly and ingenious Mr. Arthur Young, "a thouſand pounds and do you make them the *leſs* poor? By no means, but *more* ſo. Leſſen the ſpur to induſtry in a claſs that muſt be maintained by induſtry, and you take away what nothing can recompence." Should we therefore allow what our author contends for, that rights of common are not charged with any equivalent rent, and that they are, as in the caſes now ſtated, and doubtleſs in many others, in themſelves alone, a real and certain benefit to the poor; yet would he be far from having proved that they render them ſo eaſy and comfortable as they might be from that trueſt ſource of virtue and happineſs, the conſtant efforts of their own regular induſtry. *(b)*

(b) See Mr. Young's Annals of Agriculture, No. 27, p. 221.

2. *Objection to Enclosures from the rambling Disposition of Sheep.*

"IT is a circumstance universally known and "acknowledged, we are informed, p. 61, that "sheep are of a very *roving* nature, and never "thrive well in a state of confinement, however "good their pasture; and so fond are they of *change*, "that they will quit a good pasture for a bad one; "consequently if there were no commons, for the "farmers to turn their sheep upon in the spring, "when their grounds are shut up to secure the "summer crop, they would not keep any thing like "the quantity of sheep in the summer which they "could very well maintain in the winter." When our author was about it, I wonder he did not complete the matter, and acquaint us that sheep are of so singular a constitution, that they thrive much better *without* food than *with* it. For it is notorious that enclosures, properly managed, produce three times as much pasture as mere wastes and commons; it is, therefore, somewhat hard if the farmer cannot contrive to keep an equal number of sheep both summer and winter, as if he were to turn his rich fields into barren heaths.

But "sheep it seems are of so *roving* a nature, "that they never thrive in a long state of confinement." If this be really true, to any considerable

able degree, they muſt be totally different from all other animals reared for human food, which generally thrive beſt when ſtill and quiet, and contented with their ſituation. Nay, the very circumſtance of *houſed lambs*, and the rapidity with which they fatten, does it not ſuggeſt the idea that even full grown ſheep ſupplied with proper food, might be likewiſe expeditiouſly and effectually fattened under equal confinement?

Beſides, to keep our author's reaſoning full in view, what is the confinement neceſſarily reſulting from encloſures? May not ſeparate fields and paſtures contain from five to fifty acres, of almoſt every form and figure? Will not the prudent farmer change his ſheep from one to the other, ſo as to give them as great variety as poſſible? And will not this afford ample indulgence to their rambling diſpoſition? I ſee no manner of reaſon why the poor creatures, with empty bellies and mournful cries, ſhould gallop ten or twenty miles a day over a barren heath, in queſt of a wretchedly precarious ſubſiſtence, inſtead of lying down calm and content and fed to the full; unleſs, indeed, it were intended to keep them in excellent breathing that they might at length figure away at Newmarket, or ſome other of our public race grounds.

3. *Objections from Soil, and Situation.*

That there are ſoils and ſituations incapable of improvement by the utmoſt efforts of human art, may ſafely be granted. "I am far from thinking," ſays Mr. B. Pryce of Saliſbury, "every com-"mon would pay for encloſing, and admit of the "ſame cultivation as the adjoining lands. But I "verily believe that four parts in five of the com-"mons throughout the kingdom are capable of "great improvement; either by encloſing or al-"lotting into ſpecific ſhares; by planting, drain-"ing, cleanſing, or by ſuch management as the "different ſoils, ſituations and circumſtances re-"ſpectively require, and which they are debarred "from in their preſent ſtate. Such improvements "I am well convinced would be highly beneficial "both to individuals and to ſociety." No rational advocate for encloſures ever wiſhed to extend the practice further than this. Let us ſee how the matter ſtands reſpecting the ſoils, &c. ſpecified by our author.

"Many extenſive waſtes," ſays he, p. 49, "ſuch "as Saliſbury Plain, Newmarket Heath, Odſey "Heath, &c. being a chalk, rocky ſoil, are ut-"terly incapable of improvement by cultivation. "In their preſent uncncloſed ſtate they maintain "large breeding flocks of ſheep, whence they are

"folded

" folded upon the neighbouring ploughed lands, " which by that means alone are rendered fertile."

That heaths impart fertility to the neighbouring enclosures is, I believe, not very usual. On the contrary, who has not frequently beheld the barren debilitated condition of those lands which are situate upon the borders of an extensive common? Mr. Pryce just now mentioned, a man of very accurate and extensive observation in these matters, in a letter dated the 2d of January, 1787, to a friend who has favoured me with the sight of it, says, " You remember calling on me at Chard- " stock, near Axminster, last summer, when I " was valuing that extensive manor, where there " are upwards of a thousand acres of common- " able lands. I have before remarked, and it ap- " peared very striking upon that survey, that " the *enclosed lands*, on those estates where the " occupiers depend most upon the common rights, " are greatly impoverished. The reason of which " is, that a larger stock being kept than can be " conveniently maintained, every blade of grass, " that the enclosed land produces, is annually " mowed for the support of the cattle in winter. " The dung of these cattle, is lost upon the commons, " instead of being returned to the enclosed land; " which, by this wretched system, becomes much " impoverished and exhausted, to the great preju- " dice

" dice of the land owner, the occupier and the
" community."

But granting that ploughed lands are ſometimes benefited by ſheep being folded upon them from the adjoining commons, might not this advantage, to a much more conſiderable degree, and with greater convenience, be derived from ſuch commons when encloſed? Grant they are improper to be broken up and ſubjected to tillage; might not the farmer from the clover and artificial graſſes of his arable lands *fold* upon them, and thereby produce a more rich and abundant herbage? And might he not hence in return more profitably fold his arable lands, and thereby render both of them doubly productive? Certainly he might; nor would any evil reſult from it, but that his wool would be coarſer nearly in proportion to the increaſed richneſs of his paſture.

This evil, it muſt be acknowledged would probably follow; (*a*) as it certainly has followed from ſome of the encloſures already made. Fine wool is much more ſcarce, and of courſe conſiderably dearer, than it was before they took place.

(*a*) Mr. Arthur Young, in his annals of Agriculture, has given an exception to this; and Mr. Stone, (page 66 of his Suggeſtions, &c.) aſſures us that Mr. Bakewell of Diſhley in Lincolnſhire, by due attention to his breed, can produce wool of almoſt what degree of fineneſs he pleaſes. This requires further proof.

Should all our paſtures, were ſuch a thing poſſible, be rendered as luxuriant as thoſe of Lincolnſhire, Leiceſterſhire, &c our ſheep would all, in a courſe of years, become of ſimilar bulk with thoſe there produced.

No longer ſhould we ſee thoſe nimble, dapper little creatures which now appear on the South Downs of Suſſex, on Newmarket Heath, or the poorer grounds of Suffolk and Norfolk; nor ſhould we any more poſſeſs that fine wool we at preſent boaſt. But whatever were loſt in *quality*, would be amply ſupplied in *quantity*, and *ſhillings* gained inſtead of *pence*.

The ingenious Mr. Anderſon informs us that the ſheep fed on the poor lands of Scotland in the neighbourhood of Aberdeen produced wool of ſo delicate a texture that a pair of ſtockings were made of it which might be drawn through a common gold ring; that they exceeded the richeſt ſilk, were valued at five guineas, and preſented to Marſhal Keith. *If we cannot hope to make ſuch elegant preſents* from our fertile encloſures, let us remember that a fat ox is better than a ſilk-worm; that a bale of coarſe ſerge is more valuable than a yard of fine broad cloth; and that fifty pair of yarn ſtockings and fifty fear-nothing coats, to keep warm the legs and backs of fifty poor peaſants, are in a national view, of more importance than a ſingle

N pair

pair of hoſe, though rivalling the moſt gloſſy ſilk, or than the fineſt cloth which a Scotiſh loom ever produced, or which ever graced the perſon of the ſmarteſt beau.

" But ſo thin is the ſoil of theſe commons," it ſeems, " and ſo chalky and rocky is it underneath, " that they grow no trees, and are incapable of " producing them." But is not the preſumption juſt the contrary? For, as Mr. Lamport rightly obſerves, do not the moſt bleak and rocky hills produce firs more ſolid in their timber, though ſlower in their growth, than thoſe which are planted in richer ſoils?

" There are other commons," it is ſaid, p. 51, " which are an abſolute ſand, and which produce " ſcarcely any thing but heath, wild thyme, &c. " affording very little ſuſtenance even for ſheep. " Such for inſtance as Eſher and Cobham com- " mons, and part of Windſor Foreſt, Bagſhot " Heath, &c. If upon a ſurvey there ſhould be " found, at an eaſy diſtance, marle or other ſtiff " earth to mix with the ſand, it would probably " be a public benefit if they were encloſed and " cultivated." It certainly would, nor need we deſpair of this, even though marle and ſtiff earth to mix with the ſand ſhould *not* be found at an *eaſy* diſtance. For by means of navigable canals, might not ſuitable manure, with very little difficulty, be

conveyed

conveyed from any diſtance? A hundred miles as well as one? And is there a barren ſpot in the kingdom which has not its correſpondent manure within that compaſs?

Navigable canals appear abſolutely neceſſary to the full perfection of the agriculture of this kingdom whether in the new or the old encloſures. The objections to them I have hitherto heard, and conſidered in a general view; whatever force they may have in ſome local applications, ſeem to me, when fairly examined, to be of very little weight. It is ſaid they are often a violation of private property, and that they ſometimes impair the beauty of gentlemen's eſtates. Particular injuries are eaſily compenſated, and as to the mere charms of fine views, and delightful proſpects, navigable canals more frequently tend to heighten than to diminiſh them, not only by means of that various ſhifting ſcene they immediately introduce, but by that richer luxuriance of paſturage and thoſe higher improvements of culture, which they finally accompliſh. —And as to the apprehenſion that they will leſſen the national ſecurity by decreaſing the number of ſeamen, it ſtrikes me as the moſt groundleſs objection of all. The event would be juſt the reverſe. Not a fiſh, not a coal, (*f*) the leſs would be carried to

(*f*) A plan has lately been publiſhed of a navigable canal to be made from Lynn to London, through the counties of Norfolk,

to London, or to any other of our ports, a very few of them indeed excepted; while ten times the quantity of both would be conveyed not only to most of our inland counties, but to the internal parts of the maritime ones; and thus two thirds of our people would be furnished with the first necessaries of life, food and fuel, at little more than half the price they are now. This increased consumption of fish would proportionably multiply the number of fishermen; this augmented consumption of coals would equally augment the num-

folk, Suffolk, and Essex. But it does not appear to have gained that degree of attention which either the importance of the subject, or the ingenuity with which it has been treated, might justly claim. I have seldom met with a scheme, as far as I am able to judge, of greater plausibility, or more apparently replete with beneficial consequences. The ingenious author has, I believe, among other advantages, hinted at the diminution of expence it would occasion in the carriage of coals; but it seems to have escaped him, that the expediency of this is daily increasing, from the perpetual decrease of our wood, and the approaching necessity of burning almost entirely this species of fuel. Many of the farmers as well as tradesmen, in a great measure do so already; and, in the course of thirty years, they will all not improbably be obliged to do the same, together with even the poor themselves. How heavy a burthen this will be is not difficult to estimate, when it is remembered that the carriage alone to many places is now 18 or 20s. a chaldron, nearly the original price of the coals; whereas, should the projected canal be made, to no place would it exceed five or six.

ber of colliers, both in the mine and upon the coaſt; who being, as it were ſailors in embryo, would man our future navies, and "carry protection or "terror as far as waters roll, or winds could waft "them." In a word, *encloſures, navigable canals, agriculture, our fiſheries, and our naval ſtrength ſeem inſeparably united.* The three laſt will be the natural conſequence of the two firſt; and while we exert ourſelves to make them go hand in hand, no bounds need to be ſet to the fertility of our ſoil, the increaſe of our people, or the power, proſperity and glory of Great Britain.

4. *General Review of a Pamphlet entitled* "CURSORY REMARKS UPON ENCLOSURES, BY A COUNTRY FARMER."

HAVING examined our author's leading positions, and likewise considered his several miscellaneous objections, I should here have concluded. But since writing the greater part of the preceding pages a new publication has made its appearance intitled *Cursory Remarks on Enclosures, by a Country Farmer*. As the writer we have already attended to chiefly directs his arguments against the enclosure of *waste lands*, this gives a dreadful list of the consequences of enclosing *common fields*. He asserts, (*a*) that although the farmer of an enclosure can use his land as he pleases, and has the strongest motives to cultivate and improve it to the utmost, yet that his corn will be neither so much in quantity nor so good in quality (*b*) as that which grows in the open fields; that all near the hedges will be thin and weak; and yet, that thin and weak as it is, the hedges being, we must suppose, necessarily as high as the walls of Babylon, it will so retain the wet, and be made so extremely soft by a shower of rain, or the very dews of heaven, that neither sun nor wind

(*a*) P. 9, 10. (*b*) P. 11. (*c*) P. 2.

can

can either dry or harden it; that a few grains thus ſoaked will ſo mar the whole, that the poor baker will be forced to ſpoil our bread with alum, or feed the hogs with his flour; that the kingdom has by encloſures loſt two hundred and fifty thouſand inhabitants, the greater part of whom have migrated to foreign countries, and, that, although moſt of them were previouſly reduced to a moſt dreadful ſtate of poverty, they yet carried away with them two millions and a half of money (*d*), and thereby enabled the Americans to defeat the Britiſh troops, (*e*) and ſecure their independence; that they notwithſtanding left behind them an amazing multitude of miſerable wretches, ſtarving for want of employment; which employment, however, we are carefully informed, many of them were unable to perform if they could have got it, they being already worn out with age and infirmity; that the reſt, deſtitute of courage to croſs the ocean, have turned thieves and robbers at home, and filled the country with plunder and rapine: In a word, that if this practice of encloſing is ſuffered to go on, England muſt be content with *about half* (*f*) its number of inhabitants; that although encloſures of the moſt diſadvantageous kind do not indeed diminiſh proviſions in the ſame proportion as they diminiſh the mouths which are to conſume them, and although ſuch proviſions are raiſed at leſs expence, yet

(*d*) P. 8. (*e*) P. 7. (*f*) P. 22.

has

has their price neceſſarily encreaſed from the encreaſe of encloſures. Such are the various vague inconſiſtent reaſonings of this writer, which, thus collected together and placed in one view, may very ſafely be left to deſtroy themſelves.

I would, however, juſt obſerve, that it is only to *one* of his great and leading aſſertions, namely *the tendency of encloſures to depopulate*, that he has given the evidence of *fact*, and that that too is merely of a *ſingle* pariſh; whereas, in my *Enquiry concerning the Influence which Encloſures have had upon the Population of this Kingdom*, I have given 90 pariſhes recently incloſed, which, notwithſtanding many of them have doubtleſs been miſmanaged, ſome been converted to paſture, which would have done better in tillage, and others put under the plough which would have been more profitable if grazed; have yet, upon the whole, not only greatly encreaſed their people, but even conſiderably more increaſed them than thoſe pariſhes that have not been recently encloſed.

Beſides, the ſingle inſtance which this writer has given, is that of a pariſh in which common fields of arable land have been turned into paſture, which, the warmeſt advocates for encloſures readily allow diminiſh the inhabitants upon that particular ſpot; and we are not unwilling to acknowledge that even 50, or 100, perhaps more, ſuch pariſhes are to be

found

found in the kingdom; and yet we confidently maintain that the result of the whole is a greatly augmented population.

CONCLUSION.

TO resume our general subject, both speculation and experience concur to establish the utility and expedience of enclosures. Indeed the advantages arising from them, in every view, are so various and almost infinite, that I am really surprised that enemies to them can still remain; yet more astonished am I that these enemies should be found among *Englishmen*. *Englishmen* boast the high privilege of independence, the invaluable liberty of converting their private possessions, each man for himself, to the greatest advantage, unconnected with the whims, unsubjected to the fancies and encroachments of those around them. But who can be thus *independent*, who can be thus at *liberty*, while he joins in the restrained cultivation of open fields, or shares in the precarious profits of wastes and commons? That I may not however further enlarge upon the subject myself, (to which a deep conviction of its importance towards the advancement of our agriculture, towards the increase of our national wealth, population and prosperity strongly inclines me,) I will here take my leave of it nearly in the animated words of my obliging and spirited correspondent of Longleat.

" I beg leave to aſk, ſays he, the following " queſtions, and when they are anſwered ſatisfacto- " rily, the public will be able to judge for them- " ſelves.

" Is it not evident that the inhabitants of this " kingdom are greatly increaſed? Is it not equally " manifeſt that the conſumption of all kinds of " proviſions is increaſed ſtill more than our peo- " ple? Is not wheaten bread the univerſal food of " the loweſt orders of men in counties where it uſed " to be confined to the middle and higher ranks? " Is not that bread made of the fineſt flour? Is " not the conſumption of cheeſe and butter, in " many places, almoſt trebled? Are not beef and " mutton now eaten almoſt daily in villages where " formerly the uſe of them was hardly known, or " not more than once a week? Do not the farmers, " in moſt parts of the nation, allow their ſervants, " and workmen three times as much ſtrong beer as " heretofore? Muſt not this have vaſtly aug- " mented the conſumption of barley? At the ſame " time, are there not thouſands of quarters both of " that and of wheat diſtilled more than uſed to be?

" How has this increaſed conſumption been " ſupplied, but by an increaſe of produce? Whence " has ariſen this increaſe of produce, but from an " increaſe in the *extent*, and ſtill more, amend- " ment in the *mode* of the cultivation of our lands?

" Is

" Is it not for the intereſt of the community
" that the greateſt poſſible produce ſhould be
" obtained from every acre of ground, and that
" each acre ſhould be applied to the propereſt uſe
" for which nature deſigned it ?

" Have not the improvements of late years, by
" the uſe of lime, chalk, marle, &c. and by the
" culture of turnips, clover, ſaintfoin, &c. ren-
" dered thoſe *high* and *light* lands abundantly pro-
" ductive which before were of little or no value ?
" And as to the *low* and *heavy* ones, has not the
" general introduction of draining been the means
" of converting cold, wet arable to dry, healthy
" paſture, and of rendering many thouſand acres
" of boggy, unwholeſome meadow ſound and pro-
" per for breeding and fatting cattle, on which
" it was before impoſſible they ſhould be either
" fatted or bred ? In theſe ſeveral caſes, have not
" the rents been doubled, trebled, and even quadru-
" pled ? And muſt not the produce have been
" enlarged in full proportion to enable the farmer
" to pay ſuch heightened rents ?

" If I am anſwered in the affirmative, allow me
" to aſk, how could theſe things have been accom-
" pliſhed, unleſs the common fields and paſtures
" had been divided and allotted in ſpecific ſhares
" to every proprietor, ſo that he might have it in
" his power to manage his land in that way which
" nature

" nature intended, and in which, his own expe-
" rience taught him, it would be most produc-
" tive and profitable ?

" If I am answered in the negative, then, in God's name, let all the ancient enclosures, as well as the new, be again thrown open. Let us no longer boast of our improvements, but let us return to our primitive barbarity, and let our flocks and herds resume the undisturbed possession of the forests. No longer let William the Norman be branded in history for throwing down the enclosures of a few villages to enlarge his forest. We are now told (in what we were foolish enough to think the enlightened age of George III.) that he stopt his hand too soon; for that it is by forests alone we can find subsistence, and that the destruction of them, and the destruction of the kingdom are inseparable."

F I N I S.
